Other Books by MIE Publishing

*They Also Served*

*Secrets of Finding Unclaimed Money*

*How to Locate Anyone Who Is or Has Been in the Military*

# Find Anyone Fast

Third Edition

Richard S. Johnson

Debra Johnson Knox

MIE PUBLISHING

MIE Publishing is a subsidiary of Military Information Enterprises, Inc.

Printed in the United States of America.



MIE Publishing
PO Box 17118
Spartanburg, SC 29301
(800) 937-2133
E-mail: information@militaryusa.com
*http://www.militaryusa.com*

Library of Congress Cataloging-in-Publication Data:
Johnson, Richard S. (1933-)
Find anyone fast/ Richard S. Johnson, Debra Johnson Knox,
—3rd ed.

p. cm.
Includes index,
ISBN 1-877639-85-0
1. Missing persons—Investigation—United States—Handbooks, manuals, etc. 2. Public records—United States—Handbooks, manuals, etc. I. Knox, Debra Johnson, 1964-II. Title.
HV6762.U5 J64 2001 2001030428
363.2'336--dc 21 CIP

**Dedication**

This edition is dedicated to my father,

Lt. Col. Richard S. Johnson,
June 20, 1933 – February 2, 1999,

the original author and inspiration for this book.
Thank you Dad for your love and for your service
to your country.

—Debra Johnson Knox

## Disclaimer

This book is designed to provide information and is sold with the understanding that the publisher and authors are not engaged in rendering legal or other professional services.

Every effort has been made to make this book as complete and accurate as possible. There may be mistakes, either typographical or in content. Therefore, this book should be used as a general guide.

The authors or MIE Publishing shall have neither liability nor responsibility to any person regarding any loss or damage caused or alleged to be caused directly or indirectly by the information contained in this book.

## Preface

Most folks don't realize just how easy and inexpensive it can be to find someone. Some cases may take more time and effort than others, but there are very few people you can't locate. This is especially true today because of the incredible, growing amount of information available in public records and numerous national databases. If you know where to look, anyone—even an eight-year-old—can find anyone fast!

Who's looking for these "missing" people? Each case is different. Here's a list of some likely searchers:

- family members
- adoptees in search of their natural parents
- former lovers, old friends, military and college buddies
- reunions (school, family or military)
- alumni groups
- civic, patriotic, veterans, and historical organizations
- genealogical researchers
- former spouses who are due alimony or child support
- creditors
- searchers for missing heirs to estates
- state agencies and businesses that hold abandoned money or assets
- people seeking the owners of oil and mineral rights
- people seeking the owners of real estate or property they wish to purchase
- attorneys seeking witnesses for court cases
- journalists and authors
- law enforcement agencies seeking fugitives, victims or witnesses
- federal, state and county agencies who are due taxes
- medical agencies and organizations in need of medical information or other important data
- businesses attempting to update their mailing lists
- numerous other people and organizations

## *Table of Contents*

# *How to Use This Book*

In many cases, any single technique listed in this book will lead directly to the person you're looking for. But sometimes it's not just a one-step process; you may have to use several of the techniques we've outlined for you. We suggest that you read through the whole book first. It's an easy read. And who knows, maybe you'll decide to find other people after you learn some of our strategies. Some of the concepts may be new to you, so don't resist the urge to read any of the chapters twice or three times. Unless you're reading aloud to someone, nobody will know the difference.

Each chapter of this book deals with specific steps you may need to know to find someone. Chapter 1 gives you some great case histories and other useful information that can inspire and encourage you. Chapter 2 will show you what information to collect, what methods to use for keeping records, and the attitudes necessary for successful searching.

We hope you *don't* find the person by reading Chapter 3 because that chapter explains how to find out if the person is deceased. We'll help you get the most out of that computer of yours in Chapter 4. Chapter 5 will amaze you when you see how many great databases are out there on the Internet.

In Chapter 6 we'll walk you through a variety of proven methods for finding adoptees or birth parents. And Chapter 7 is jam-packed with information on how to check someone's background using public records, maybe even someone you don't want to find.

Chapter 8 covers how to find a person who has been in the military. Chapter 9 gives all the miscellaneous resources that otherwise would slip through the cracks, especially lots of good federal resources. And finally, Chapter 10 explains how to solve the really difficult cases such as homeless people, those who live overseas, those who are in jail, and the ones who intentionally try hard not to be found

Appendix A gives useful state resources, and Appendix B covers the National Archives and Records Administration.

Appendix C shows how to request information from the U.S. government. The Freedom of Information Act enables you to get a lot of great information about people who have interacted with the federal government—including those who were in the armed services. The problem is, the same law requires you to submit the request in a very specific manner. We'll show you how to navigate through the sea of bureaucracy, and we even provide a sample letter. Even better, we've provided a copy of the Standard Form 180 you can use to make that request for military records.

In Appendix D we show you how to read a Social Security number and magically zero in on the state someone was in when his card was issued. Appendix E shows how to use locator services. And finally in Appendix F we give you a huge list of helpful books. Oh, and don't forget the glossary in the very back in case you don't understand some of the words or terms.

Some important tips: Use common sense and be persistent. Learn to be a good listener. Review your work from time to time and check everything you previously tried. Don't be afraid to ask questions or to redo your work. Review this book again to be sure you didn't miss any leads. When you're hot on someone's trail, keep after him while the information is fresh. Remember, most people are easy to locate. And difficult cases become easier if you're positive, persistent, patient and polite.

No matter who you are or who you are looking for, the methods in this book will help you Find Anyone FAST!

Chapter 1

# Case Studies

As much as you'd like it to happen, you can't find someone by wishing—you'll have to get off the couch and start looking. And while there are probably a dozen ways you could find any one person, the goal of this book is to help you find the person in the most efficient and inexpensive manner.

In theory, you could knock on every door, call every phone number, post notices on every telephone pole in every neighborhood in the United States and, sure enough, you will probably find that person. Of course, by the time you find him, you may have forgotten why you were looking. Old age does that to a person.

Or you could use the most incredible new databases or CD-ROMs, or follow the public records from his birth certificate to his marriage certificate to the deed of his first house, then his second, then his third. After that, you can trace his forwarding address through a national service, pull his current voter registration, confirm it by looking at the deed, and then knock on his door saying, "Chuck! It's me, Fred. Haven't seen you in 45 years. I'll bet you're wondering how I found you, huh?"

Then you'll feel terrible when he says, "I knew you'd find me, Fred. That's why I always list my address and phone number in the phone book!" That's when you quickly change the subject and ask him if he ever got married.

When you read the case studies in this chapter, you'll get a feel for the logical steps that some successful searchers have taken. You'll see how to locate someone by yourself using only the suggestions in this book. In other cases, you'll see how people did as much as their energy, time or resources would allow, and then they turned to professionals to make the final assault.

As we describe the scenarios here, you might want to put the book down before you read each ending, and imagine what steps you might take given the circumstances and the information available in the beginning.

We've changed some of the names here—you know, privacy and all. By the way, if you succeed in your search using the resources in this book, please write and let us know. We might want to feature you in a later edition.

## Looking for Dad in All the Wrong Places

When Brenda gave birth to her second child, she decided it was finally time to locate the father she had never met—the man who was also now the grandfather of her children. She was hoping they could at least see each other, and maybe even develop a relationship.

Her mother had divorced the man while she was pregnant with Brenda. Fortunately, her mother encouraged Brenda to look for him and was even willing to help.

Her mother knew the man's name, but not his date of birth, Social Security number, parents' names or any of his friends. She did, however, know the address of the church in Santa Barbara where they were married, and she knew the address where they briefly lived some 90 miles south in Burbank. Problem is, Brenda and all her family lived in Texas.

Where would you start? What could you do with the information at hand? Think about it for a minute.

Brenda believed she could only find him by taking a two-week vacation and driving to California, her mother at her side and the two toddlers tagging behind in the back seat.

They consulted with no one before the journey—they just relied on luck or fate. By the end of the first week, they hadn't learned anything except that they weren't doing too well. They went to the address in Burbank to find an office building where the apartment once was and no other houses or apartments in sight.

They stopped in at the Pasadena Public Library and asked the reference librarian to have mercy on them. Could she possibly help? After helping them look in old phone books and city directories to no avail, she gave them the phone number of a local man who searched for people. They left a desperate message on his answering machine and decided to keep searching until he got back to them.

They drove to Santa Barbara in hopes of finding the chapel where her mother had married her father. It was no longer there and none of the current neighbors knew what became of anyone who was associated with the church. Frustrated, they called the man who searched for people again and finally reached him. He told them to go to the Santa Barbara County Courthouse, buy a copy of the marriage certificate and drive back to Burbank, a much more likely place to find information.

Where do you imagine he was going to have them search?

When the Los Angeles County offices opened up the next morning, the three split up to search for different types of files. Brenda pored over marriage records in the recorder's office hoping to find that maybe he remarried. No record. Her mother went though the indices at the Superior Court looking for divorce files, civil cases, criminal cases or even a probate file in his name (which would indicate he had passed away). She found a civil lawsuit from many years earlier that he had filed against a client who had not paid him for work done. That could prove to be helpful.

She also found a criminal case where he had been arrested for allegedly paying some teenagers to stand outside a voter polling place and say nasty things about a candidate he didn't like. It offered a few leads and a hint of his personality.

But the leads would prove to be unnecessary. Their people-finding expert had decided to check the death certificate index at the recorder's office. When he didn't find a record there, he wisely looked in the statewide death index. It was there he found the information he knew Brenda feared—her father had died in another county in California back when she was only ten years old.

*Tools, tips and techniques that worked*: The statewide death index had the information all along. So did the Social Security Administration Death Index. If he hadn't died, the leads they found in the civil and criminal case files would possibly have led to other clues. They could also have checked with the county assessor to learn the names of former neighbors. If they had located any former neighbors, they might have gathered other clues.

*Mistakes*: They should never have left home without first gathering more personal identifying information and checking by phone, fax, modem or mail. For example, the Social

Security Death Index is available free of charge at many libraries and at LDS churches.

*High-tech solutions*: With today's technology, much can be accomplished by computer. As this book explains, computer searching is certainly the wave of the future. Brenda could have easily accessed the Internet at home or at a local library and checked Ancestry's Internet site for the Social Security Master Death Index *(www.ancestry.com)*. This would have saved her lots of time and money.

## That Old Pal of Mine

While he was on R&R in Hawaii in the middle of his Army tour in Vietnam, Steve had a date with Linda, a Red Cross worker who spoke with an accent that was strangely familiar to him. She said she was from Pennsylvania. That baffled Steve because he had never been east of the Mississippi. All through dinner Steve wracked his brain to figure out who in his life had a similar accent. Finally, as Linda was about to get in an airport-bound taxi, it dawned on him. Linda's accent was just like that of his high school friend, Rich Carson.

"Where was he born?" Linda asked.

"Pennsylvania," Steve remembered. "No wonder you have the same accent."

"What city in Pennsylvania?"

"I don't remember," Steve told her. "All I remember is he tried to talk me into going to a college near where he was from—Westminster College."

"That's in New Castle," she said. "That's where I live. Rich Carson? Did he have a brother named Louie?"

"As a matter of fact he did."

"Sure, I remember Rich. I dated Louie for awhile."

When Steve left for a tour in Vietnam, his high school buddy Rich was flipping burgers at the local Big Boy Restaurant. But when he returned, he couldn't find Rich anywhere—nor his parents, his brother or anyone. Ironically, Steve stayed in touch with Linda on and off for years. He even visited her in New Castle when he was in the area a few years later.

Fifteen years later, Steve bought a book on how to find people, followed most of the instructions, but couldn't find Rich on file anywhere in the county. The only thing he found was a very old, previously canceled voter registration affidavit that indicated Rich had moved out of the county. Steve asked the clerk if there was any way to determine which county he may have moved to. She pulled out a separate index that had forwarding addresses listed. She gave Steve the newer address in a city 150 miles away.

After finding no phone listings in the new county, Steve called that county's registrar of voters to learn that Rich had moved out of that county and left no forwarding address.

Steve then contacted his state's motor vehicle department to learn that Rich's drivers license had expired and the last address on file was the same as the one Steve already had. Steve asked the clerk at the motor vehicle department if there was any more information in the file that might help him find his friend.

"Well," the clerk said, "the file shows that he surrendered his license to the motor vehicle department in Pennsylvania. Does that help?"

You bet! Steve knew where to look. He called directory assistance for New Castle and found a listing for Rich. He called and they chatted, reminisced and eventually got together when Steve was in Pennsylvania to attend a wedding.

*Tools, tips and techniques that worked*: Steve followed the path almost flawlessly. He was especially smart to ask clerks in the registrar of voter's office and the motor vehicle department if there might be more information he didn't ask for.

*Mistakes*: Did you already figure this one out? When Steve found no record of Rich in the county, he should have immediately asked himself where Rich was likely to have moved. Hadn't Rich talked of going to college in New Castle? One quick phone call to New Castle would have worked—even though Rich never went to Westminster College and didn't return to New Castle for many years. Steve would have saved time and a sizable phone bill.

*High-tech solutions*: There are several professional computer searches that could have saved Steve many hours of work: address update search, driver's license search, or date of birth search. Any of these would have resulted in Rich's current address. The least expensive of these searches is the address update—right around $40. The address update search can be run with a former address that is up to ten years old.

## Looking for Ol' What's-Her-Name

It had been more than 20 years since Frank had spoken with Susan, a woman he had dated long before he was married. Now he was divorced. He remembered that she was divorced when he first met her, and heard that she married again after they lost touch. In fact, someone had told him she had been married at least two more times. But Frank could not, for the life of him, remember either the last name she was using when they dated or the name of the man she later married. He remembered her maiden name had been Veraldi and she was born in Italy. He wasn't sure if her parents were living in the United States.

He turned to an investigator friend for some advice. His friend asked if he could think of anything at all that he might have known about the man she married after Frank and she parted ways.

All he could remember was that he had been a football player for the nearby university but that was also many years ago. He thought he remembered that the last name was Italian, it had three or more syllables, and it may have started with the letter "P."

He called the admissions and records office at the university but found no one who could help him. Then he called the university library and asked the reference librarian for advice. She offered to let him look through the yearbooks but suggested that since he was a football player, maybe the sports department would know.

The people at the sports department were willing to go out of their way to look at the football team rosters. They read every name that seemed to fit the parameters until they found "Penunura." That was it—Jim Penunura.

Frank then checked voter registration records—first in his own county and then in surrounding counties. Sure enough, a Jim Penunura, seemingly the right age, was living in the next county. The phone number was listed on the affidavit, so he called. No answer. For two days, no answer.

He didn't want to make the 100-mile drive to the distant city, so he asked all his friends if they had any friends or contacts in that city. Sure enough, a man he worked with knew the editor of that small city's newspaper. His co-worker called the editor and asked if she ever remembered hearing the name Jim Penunura. She said she believed she remembered hearing the last name. She checked her clip files and found a story written two years earlier about a Judy Penunura marrying a Spanish man and moving with her new husband, Roberto Salinas, to his hometown of Bilbao, Spain. It mentioned her father's name, Jim Penunura. The article said the groom's family owned a large department store in Spain. The editor had a reverse directory and was able to give Frank the phone numbers of Jim Penunura's neighbors.

Frank called the neighbors to learn that Jim was out of town for at least a month—they had no idea where.

Where would you go from here?

Frank didn't feel like waiting a month for Jim to return, so he called on another friend who spoke Spanish. They checked the time zone differences with a phone operator and, at the proper time, made a conference call to the international operator and asked for Roberto Salinas in Bilbao, Spain. There were more than 20 such listings, the operator in Spain said, but she was only allowed to give out two phone numbers per call. Frank took the two and called both, but no one answered at either.

They realized they would have to make at least ten operator-assisted calls to Spain if they hoped to find the right Roberto. What they needed was someone who would read to them all the Roberto Salinas listings from the Bilbao telephone directory. Who would have access to a telephone directory in Bilbao, Spain? The answer was easy—anyone in Bilbao with a telephone. They took one of the numbers the operator had given them, changed one digit and dialed direct.

His Spanish-speaking friend asked the woman who answered if she'd be kind enough to go to her telephone directory and read to them all the listings with the name of Roberto Salinas. He added that they were looking for the Salinas family that might own a department store there.

"La familia Salinas es la duena de El Almacen Salinas en La Avenida de la Liberdad," the woman said. The friend translated.

"She says the Salinas family owns the Salinas Department Store on Liberty Avenue." The helpful Spanish woman kindly looked up the number and gave it to them.

"We're trying to get in touch with Roberto Salinas," he said to the woman who answered at the department store. In a moment, Roberto was on the line. When they told him they were looking for his wife, he gave them his unlisted home number.

Now Frank called and talked to Judy. She was reluctant to give out her mother's new last name. She said her mother was living in Utah. "Let me write to my grandmother in Denver and get my mom's phone number. I'll write to you with the information if Mom says it's okay."

Frank was too impatient, and besides, maybe Grandma would say no. He called directory assistance for Veraldi listings in Denver. Only one.

"Mrs. Veraldi? I'm an old friend of Susan's. I just talked to Judy in Spain. She said you'd give me Susan's phone number in Utah."

"Sure," she said. "Here it is."

*Tools, tips and techniques that worked*: Frank's investigator friend knew the importance of trying to recall seemingly unimportant details—in this case, the football connection. Frank's own persistence paid off when he refused to be put off by the university administration. It's almost a secret, unwritten code that school bureaucrats will feign ignorance or lack of personnel. Frank succeeded because he went around them—he checked with the reference librarian. A reference librarian is the one government employee who, even after 30 years on the job, still loves the task at hand—to find information. Even when she couldn't find the information, she at least suggested a referral. It worked.

In many areas, you can telephone the local registrar of voters for verification that someone votes. If they tell you there's no record, you know to check other areas. Frank did the correct thing by calling the registrars in nearby counties.

Frank also proved to be just impatient enough to think about other options. The best people-finders look for alternate routes while the trail is fresh and the passion is hot. At the time, he didn't know that Jim Penunura would be gone for a month. But his impatience sent him looking for alternate routes. In this case, he asked himself the all-important question, "Who would know?" He didn't need to immediately find someone who knew Jim, just someone who knew somebody in Jim's community. You may say he was lucky to find someone who knew the newspaper editor, but remember: luck is the residue of design. It doesn't come unless you plant the seeds.

Frank was brilliant to call Spain—even though he couldn't speak enough Spanish to order an enchilada combo. Most people know somebody who speaks a particular common foreign language—or they know someone who knows someone. Heck, he could have easily called any Mexican restaurant and asked if anyone there might help him with the call. And, of course, sidestepping the obstacle put up by the Spanish operator brought him even more luck to harvest.

We recommend you think twice before you misrepresent yourself or others. When Frank bypassed Judy and went straight to her grandmother, he ran the risk that Susan would be upset at Frank when she learned of his deceptive method. He was secure enough that Susan would want to talk to him that it was worth the risk. And, indeed, they were able to rekindle a wonderful flame from the past.

*Mistakes*: Frank might have asked his Spanish-speaking friend to ask for a Salinas Department Store right from the start. It certainly wouldn't have delayed them and, in this case, it would have saved them at least three international phone calls.

*High-tech solutions*: Frank could have started by checking a national telephone directory on CD-ROM at his nearby library. The last name "Veraldi" is such an uncommon name there couldn't be that many in the country; there was only one in Denver. And it's likely most are related. Overseas telephone numbers are available on CD-ROM and on the Internet and may have been accessible at the library.

## Seek Ye the Naysayers of John and Paul

Award-winning investigative reporter Tim Redmond, now executive editor of the *San Francisco Bay Guardian*, tells a marvelous story of how he tracked down a tough interview. He had received copies from the FBI of its investigation and extensive surveillance during the 1960s of the Beatles, and especially singer and songwriter John Lennon. Tim was particularly intrigued and amused when he looked at photographs in the file of a long-haired, hippy-looking young man with granny glasses identified as John Lennon. Tim was amused because the photo was not of John Lennon but of a much more obscure singer named David Peel.

The story he was working on required that he contact anyone who was a part of that investigation. The FBI had blacked out the names of its agents who were working on the investigation—the only name he was able to read was that of a supervisor who apparently reviewed each report. We'll call him Agent Pettijohn. Of course, the FBI refused to put Tim in touch with Agent Pettijohn, so he called a friend in Washington DC who was once a federal investigator and asked him where old FBI agents go when they're sent out to pasture. To an association of retired federal agents, he told Tim.

Ah, but could every call be this easy. Tim found the group headquartered in Washington DC and said he was trying to get in touch with Agent Pettijohn.

"Do you mean Carl Pettijohn?" the woman asked. Tim of course said it was. She told him she couldn't give out his address or phone number, however. Tim said it was no problem. He was curious, though, in what part of the country he ended up.

"Iowa," she said. "Cedar Falls, Iowa."

Tim thanked her and immediately called directory assistance in that part of Iowa. Carl Pettijohn was listed.

"Is this former FBI Agent Carl Pettijohn who supervised the investigation of singer John Lennon?" Tim asked politely.

"How'd you get my number?" he said in apparent anger. "They're not supposed to give out my phone number!"

"They didn't, sir," Tim assured him. "I got your name out of the telephone directory." After that, Tim says, Agent Pettijohn was more than willing to talk.

*Tools, tips and techniques that worked*: Using the Freedom of Information Act (FOIA) to find information about people—especially famous or dead people (because privacy issues exempt the non-famous who are still alive)—is a great tool in itself. Tim succeeded because he asked himself, "Who would know?" He came up with someone who was a logical candidate to have the answer—and he did. Tim's approach to the association person was nonthreatening and polite. And he was firm, yet polite and respectful with Agent Pettijohn.

*Mistakes*: Since Tim was able to quickly find the agent, we can't, technically, ding him for any goof-ups. That's assuming, of course, that if he didn't have the former federal agent as a contact he would have checked with the *Directory of Associations* at his local library. He would have easily found the group listed there.

*High-tech solutions*: Checking a national telephone directory on CD-ROM or the Internet would have saved a step or two here. After Tim learned the first name, he could have quickly checked a CD-ROM and found the phone number.

## The Ultimate Birthday Gift

Ida Rockwell was a very religious woman in her 50s in 1977. She was in great pain, suffering from multiple sclerosis, but she decided she was going to try to secretly locate her husband's father. Bill Rockwell had never met or even known of his father. His mother had given him his father's name, even though the migrant worker, Tom Rockwell, had left Arizona and moved on to other fields many months before the baby he conceived was born to the young Mexican-American woman he met in the cotton fields. In fact, it was a mystery if Tom Rockwell even knew he had fathered a child. She had met the handsome "gringo" during the picking season back in 1921, fallen in love with him and—well, you can figure out the rest.

The baby, Bill, would grow up to marry a beautiful, vibrant young woman named Ida and he would continue to give her the same unselfish love after she became ill as he had given her before. He had dedicated his life to making Ida as comfortable as possible.

Bill's mother was still alive in 1977 and had provided her daughter-in-law, Ida, with some information. In spite of her disease, Ida was a noted genealogist and had undertaken the task of tracking down any information she could about Tom Rockwell. She used the common tools of a genealogist—the birth, marriage and death records on file at both the state level and at various genealogy libraries, phone books, city directories and, of course, the few details her mother-in-law had recalled—that Tom's mother's name may have been Gladys and the family may have had its roots in Michigan.

And back then Ida had done an impressive search. She finally thought she had succeeded when she found a death certificate of a Thomas Rockwell who had died a few years earlier in Michigan. The death certificate listed the informant as "Gladys Rockwell, mother."

Ida had nervously called Gladys Rockwell in Michigan only to have her hopes deflated. Gladys Rockwell told Ida that it was absolutely impossible for her late son to have been the Tom Rockwell who once picked cotton in Arizona. Absolutely impossible. Ida was, as you could imagine, discouraged that she hadn't found the right family, but there was still a glimmer of hope that Bill's father might be alive. Even so, Ida had looked everywhere she could imagine.

Fifteen years later, a few years after Bill's mother passed away, Ida was now in much more pain, in a wheelchair, and suffering from failing eyesight. In spite of her physical problems, she signed up for a class at the local college on how to use public records to gather information. She was soon encouraged again and asked the instructor to review her search documents from 15 years earlier.

The instructor carefully examined each document and read Ida's notes. When he came to the Michigan death certificate of a Thomas Rockwell who had been born to a Gladys Rockwell, he asked how Ida knew for sure that this wasn't the death certificate of her father-in-law.

"Because his mother told me her son never fathered such a child," Ida told him.

"And what made you believe her?" the instructor asked.

"What made me believe her? That's simple," she said with an almost divine confidence. "Mothers don't lie. Why would she want to lie to me?"

"I know it's hard for you to consider," her instructor told her, "but not everyone is as honest as you are. Pick up your search as if you doubted that Gladys Rockwell was telling the truth."

Ida retraced her steps from 15 years earlier but found the telephone number she had written down for Gladys Rockwell was now disconnected. The reference librarian in the Michigan community, with the help of a criss-cross directory, gave her the names and addresses of people now living in Gladys's old neighborhood. A neighbor told Ida that Gladys Rockwell had moved away at least ten years earlier.

On a lark, Ida called the Michigan state vital records office and requested they search the death index for the past 15 years for a Gladys Rockwell. There was only one, so Ida used her credit card and had a copy of the certificate mailed to her in Arizona. When it arrived, it was clear that this Gladys Rockwell was the same person with whom Ida had spoken years earlier—the woman who denied that her son, Tom, was Bill Rockwell's father.

Ida searched the woman's death certificate for clues. There was an address listed as the place where Gladys Rockwell had been living and also as the place where Gladys had died. And the person listed as the informant used that same address. Her name was Janice Heath. Her phone number was listed with directory assistance at that address.

Ida called Janice Heath and learned that she runs a boarding house with many elderly guests. Yes, she remembered Gladys Rockwell living and dying there. When Ida recounted the story of Gladys's denial 15 years earlier, Janice Heath told her that, knowing Gladys, there was a good chance she had been lying. "You should talk to her son, Arnold," she said. "He'd be the one who would know."

"We've been hoping all our lives we'd hear from that baby my brother Tom told us he may have created in Arizona," Arnold Rockwell told a tearful Ida on the telephone. "Even on his death bed he refused to tell us the name of the woman he left behind back then."

Ida didn't wait for Bill's next birthday. When he got home from work that very night, she handed him a note that read:

"Your Uncle Arnold wants you to call him. He wants to meet you and tell you about your father."

*Tools, tips and techniques that worked*: Even with practically no information, Ida used her public records skills to ultimately locate her husband's father. She also turned to an expert to review her work and give her the right suggestions.

*Mistakes*: Obviously Ida's biggest mistake was not accurately assessing the point of view of the woman who turned out to be her husband's grandmother. Documents don't always tell the truth. Neither do people. This error set her back fifteen years. Had she not been so believing, Bill would have been able to make contact with his grandmother. And Bill's own mother may have been able to meet the family of that man who walked into and, as quickly, out of her life so many years before in the cotton fields of Arizona.

*High-tech solutions*: The Social Security Master Death Index is a terrific and accessible tool. It's available several places on the Internet (see Chapter 5) and at some libraries on CD-ROM. You can put in names and look at different ages of the people who are deceased. This would have saved a little time—but she still would have to verify that it was the right Tom Rockwell, and the family members were the only ones who knew for sure.

## My Daddy Wore Green

If you were to look at 23-year-old Vivien Giddings, you might not be able to figure out her ethnicity—or even know she has any non-European blood in her. If anything, she could pass as maybe an Italian. But Giddings is the adopted name she picked up from her stepfather, an Ohio policeman, shortly after he married her mother, the former Nguyen Thi Thu.

Vivien's real father was a G.I. who was in Vietnam in 1971 when he fell in love with the beautiful Thu, as she was known.

He was transferred back to the United States before Vivien was born and stayed in touch with Thu for only a short while. When she hadn't heard from Vivien's father for a couple of years, Thu agreed to marry another U.S. serviceman who loved them both and promised to bring them home with him. Randy Giddings kept his promise and provided a wonderful life for his new family in Pennsylvania.

When Vivien was about four, a man came to visit her mother—a man who looked at her in a way she says she never forgot. By the time she was grown, married and expecting a child of her own, she was still haunted by the belief that that man who looked at her in such a strange way was, in reality, her real father. Her mother claimed to remember no such man. But her stepfather took her aside and told her the truth about her birth father. The two men had known each other in Vietnam.

He explained to Vivien that he and her father had exchanged some harsh words and that he would probably never come back to see her. He offered, however, to help Vivien find him. Her stepfather felt sure he could use the extensive police resources and contacts he had to track down the man, Matthew Swoboda—but he failed to locate him.

Vivien went to her college library and studied up on ways of finding people. She asked her stepfather to tell her anything more he could remember about her father. He told her Matthew Swoboda was an Army pilot, but didn't remember much else.

Vivien remembered reading that the Federal Aviation Administration maintained records on all active civilian pilots. She called the FAA headquarters in Oklahoma City and asked them if there was a Matthew Swoboda listed. There was only one. He was the right age and was living in Hawaii.

Vivien was able to find a phone number there and, after

having a male friend leave him an innocuous message, he called back. He confirmed he was Vivien's father, but asked that she not call him at home. He gave his work number. She called, he talked, she cried, he promised and she believed. He told her of wonderful things he wanted to do for her when he got done with a big project he was coordinating.

But after months of waiting and calling for him, Vivien finally gave up—at least for the moment. Maybe his project ran longer than he thought, she tells people. She doesn't believe it either.

*Tools, tips and techniques that worked*: Again, asking for details will almost always give you better clues. In this case, her father was still a pilot, so she easily got the information from the FAA.

*Mistakes*: Many law enforcement people are spoiled with their government-only databases. In reality, if someone doesn't drive and doesn't get arrested, he's not going to show up on many of their computers. The average citizen has more access to legal, people-finding information than most law enforcement investigators.

*High-tech solutions*: Since her father had an unusual name, a national telephone directory on CD-ROM or the Internet could have easily and quickly given her his name and telephone number (or that of a relative). She could have accessed the pilot database on the Internet which would have given her his home address.

## A Bridge to the Dark Past

It was one of those Sunday adventures investigative journalist Don Ray enjoyed—a time to get away from the deadlines, the hounding editors, the onslaught of tipsters and whistle blowers who each hope they can catch the ear of someone in the news media who might tell their story.

He spent that particular Sunday with his friend Neal Velgos. They decided to get a close-up look at the infamous "Suicide Bridge." Don had grown up not far from the stately old Colorado Street Bridge spanning the Arroyo Seco—a hundred-foot deep, quarter-mile wide gouge that fits its Spanish translation perfectly—dry canyon. While today a high, wrought-iron fence cages the cars and pedestrians and prevents anyone from falling or jumping off, that wasn't the case during the Depression. Apparently enough people jumped to their death that it took on the name Suicide Bridge before city officials thought to install the fence.

Don and Neal took with them a 35-year-old book they'd found that described, somewhat, the bridge's checkered past. They learned that scores of people had used the bridge as a jumping-off point from life. They were especially intrigued to learn about the last two victims of the bridge in 1937. It was a young mother who first threw her three-year-old daughter off the bridge and then jumped to her own death. What intrigued the explorers was reading that the little girl had actually survived the fall. Of course, they both wanted to know what became of her.

How would you go about finding her? Remember, you don't even know her name.

The incident must have been covered by the local newspapers. Since Don and Neal didn't know the exact date, they headed for the nearest library.

The reference librarian in the history room had the file. It was labeled, "Colorado Street Bridge." In it they read newspaper stories that named the little girl, Jeannette, her mother, father, and both sets of grandparents. The story described Jeannette's mother as having been depressed over having to quit her job so that her husband could qualify for a government-sponsored job for families with low income.

Armed with the names, Neal went first to the county recorder to look for a marriage involving Jeannette. The math was fairly easy. If Jeannette was three in 1937, she was probably born in 1934. She would have turned twenty in 1954, so Neal started looking for a marriage in 1950 when she would have been sixteen.

Sure enough, he found a marriage certificate for her at a young age. Rather than track her down today using her married name, Neal surmised the marriage probably didn't last that long. And, indeed, he found a record of a divorce at the county clerk's office—a divorce that took place not too long after the marriage.

Back to the marriage index. Yes, she was married several years later—older and wiser. Neal guessed that this one might stick. Correct again. Voter records showed her living with the same husband just a few miles from the bridge.

The next morning they showed up at her door. When she answered, they asked if she was Jeannette. She said she was.

"We're working on a project that we may end up writing as a news feature," Don told her. "We're interested in the Colorado Street Bridge?"

Jeannette smiled slowly and said, "Okay, what do you boys want to know?"

"Uh, how are you? I mean, after that fall and all?"

She smiled again. "I'm fine. In spite of what the papers said, I walked away without a scratch." She said some tree branches apparently broke her fall. Then she landed on soft sand. "Why don't you come in," she said after realizing they knew much more than any burglar would need to know.

Inside, she told of how the event changed her life—how when she was a teenager, she realized she was saved for a reason and that reason was God's desire for her to help others. She was now working at a church school, helping children.

Don asked her how she had dealt with all the newspaper people who undoubtedly followed up on her throughout the years. "You boys are the first," she said.

"Funny you should be here today," she said. "Just yesterday afternoon I decided it was time to tell my daughter, for the first time, the story of what happened to me when I was a little girl." She motioned to the coffee table and the old, gray box sitting on it. She told them to open it. Inside, they found copies of all the newspaper clippings her grandmother had kept for her. The day before, she had gone into the closet and pulled the dusty box off the shelf at nearly the exact moment that Neal was pulling her dusty marriage certificate off the shelf at the county recorder's office.

Don and Neal wrote up her story—37 years later—in the Los Angeles *Times*.

*Tools, tips and techniques that worked*: Again, a reference librarian was able to speed up the search. Neal's logical searching at the county offices was nearly flawless. A nonthreatening approach made Jeannette feel safe and more willing to cooperate.

*Mistakes*: Probably the award goes to the news media who placed the little girl in the limelight and then failed to check in with her over the years.

*High-tech solutions*: Before digging, the only information at hand was the little girl's name and approximate year of birth. A date of birth computer search could have found her using her first name only and year of birth. This type of search is used often for women simply because they marry and change their last name. The search returns matches of the first name and year of birth. Of course, many names would appear on the initial print out. But then you could quickly check for any matches in that state. This would narrow it down to a smaller group which you could call by phone.

★ ★ ★ ★

No two searches are ever the same. As you can see, the most successful searches involve planning, empathy, attention to detail, organization, thoroughness, persistence, patience, impatience, passion and compassion.

We have enjoyed sharing with you these techniques, tools, tips, resources and wonderful stories we've encountered over the years.

We offer you encouragement in your search. If you get stuck along the way, we'll be happy to give you a hint that will, hopefully, get you rolling again on your way to a successful, happy encounter with someone you've been trying so hard to find.

*—Dick Johnson and Debra Johnson Knox*

# Gathering Identifying Information

You can't begin your search for a person until you have enough personal identifying information about him. You're not looking for just any John Smith. You're looking for a very specific John Smith—the one born on a certain date, in a particular location, to a specific woman, his mother, in a specific family. He has a unique Social Security number, went to specific schools, worked for specific employers, and joined specific social or professional organizations. And he has a very distinctive signature. If you know any of these things, you will eventually find him. The more identifying information you have, the easier and quicker it will be.

But it's quite easy to head off in the wrong direction and become hopelessly lost if you aren't well organized. All too often, people unwittingly make a careless wrong turn and end up chasing the wrong John Smith just because they didn't keep good records. All successful investigators are almost pathological about their notes and files. You must keep detailed, legible notes in either a computer or a notebook. If you're not sure how to organize your notes, we recommend you use our Individual Data Worksheet in Appendix C. Make a copy for each subject. Neatly write down or type every detail you uncover along the way so that, later on, you'll be able to understand what you wrote. And don't put off entering the information at the end of each search day. If you wait—even for a couple of hours—you may forget the one detail that is the key to finding the person. At the very least, you'll find yourself frustrated because you don't understand what you wrote. Write down every detail—immediately and neatly. This will save you money and time down the road.

Here are some kinds of identifying information that could help you succeed in your search:

*Names*: Complete legal name (first, middle and last), nicknames, maiden name, previous married names, and aliases.

*Personal identifying information*: Social Security number, date and place of birth, driver's license number, physical description (height, weight, hair and eye color, tattoos, scars, disabilities, etc.). A photograph can be useful. Sometimes even a copy of his signature will do the trick.

*Personal credit history*: Credit history and bankruptcy information.

*Criminal history*: Traffic violations, jail and prison records, records of arrests.

*Civil court filings*: Lawsuits, divorces, relatives' probate files, small claims court, name change actions.

*Names and addresses of relatives and friends*: Names of parents, spouse, former spouses, brothers, sisters, other relatives (aunts, uncles, cousins, etc.), children, children's spouses, and the phone numbers and addresses of where they work or live.

*Military service*: Service number, Veterans Affair's claim number, Veterans Affair's insurance number, military service branch, dates of military service, unit or ship assignments, installation or base assignments, overseas duty (Vietnam, Korea, Germany, Saudi Arabia, etc.), rank or rating (if you don't know the rank, was he enlisted or an officer?), disability, membership in veteran or military reunion organizations, membership in specific reserve or National Guard units during specific time periods.

*Property ownership*: Real estate, cars, trucks, boats, airplane, motorcycles and guns he owns, and the state in which they are registered.

*Schools*: Elementary, high school, colleges, trade schools and universities he may have attended during a specific time period. Include the subjects he may have studied, majors he may have declared and any degrees he received.

*Job-related information*: Prior jobs, labor union he may have joined, professional licenses, membership in professional organizations, names and addresses of people he once worked for or worked with.

*Social history*: Church or synagogue affiliation, membership in lodges, fraternal and service organization, names, addresses and telephone numbers of friends, political party affiliation, voter registration information, foreign and national travel history.

*Avocations and hobbies*: Special talents, things he collected, athletic activities, hunting, boating, fishing, flying, amateur radio broadcasting, motorcycle riding, etc.

*Lifestyle information*: Drinking habits, drug use, civic activities, religious activities, type of friends, etc.

Don't let all this overwhelm you. A little later in this book we'll tell you, in great detail, how to use these things.

We can't stress enough how important it is to gather as much identifying information as possible. A lot of people take off too quickly with just a little information and end up wasting a lot of time and money. They call every John Smith in every phone book across the country. You may eventually find him that way, but it would have been easier if you had first learned that the John Smith you were looking for lived on Auburn Road in Pontiac, Michigan, attended Drake University in Detroit and once worked at Big Boy Restaurant in Walled Lake. It's a lot like the guy who lost his keys in a dark parking lot and was on his hands and knees under the overhead light. A friend came along to help and asked, "Where did you lose them?" "Over there," he said, pointing to the far, dark corner of the lot. His friend asked him why he wasn't looking for them over there. "Because the light's better over here!"

Sometimes one seemingly obscure piece of information will lead you right to the person you're looking for. A colleague of ours tells the story of how, armed with only a name and a very old prior address, he was able to find a man by simply asking for more details. He called the neighbor who lived next door to the old address for a least 20 years, and asked if he knew where his former neighbor was. The man said he hadn't known his former neighbor well and couldn't be of any help. He didn't know anything about the man—when he moved, why he moved or where he had gone. But our colleague pressed him even more and asked if he remembered anything about the day his neighbor moved away.

"I told you I don't have any information for you," the man insisted. "All I know is they brought in a moving van for the furniture and a flatbed truck for that plane he was building and then they were gone." Plane he was building? One phone call to the Federal Aviation Administration was all it took to find the man's current address on his pilot's license.

Once you really get rolling on your search, you'll discover there are so many likely resources that you won't know where to look first. Right off the bat you can tap into countless sources such as family members, friends, neighbors, former bosses and fellow employees, social organizations, schools, colleges, alumni groups, veterans organizations, places of worship, libraries, government agencies from the township all the way up to the federal offices, newspaper indexes and oceans of computer databases and Internet resources. We'll tell you more about all of these in much greater detail later in the book.

And remember to think positively and don't embrace obstacles. Now that you're armed with this book you should constantly remind yourself that you're going to find that person. Your question to yourself shouldn't be, "I wonder if I'll find him?" Rather, it should be, "I wonder where he'll be when I find him?"

Keep in mind, however, that your watchwords are efficiency, persistence, and organization. And the best way to succeed is to create your own Individual Data Worksheet like the one shown in Appendix C. It will keep you on track as long as you religiously enter all the information you uncover, the minute you uncover it. It will become your road map of where you need to be going for information as well as where you've been.

Chapter 

## *Death Records*

### Is the person you're looking for even alive?

Maybe it's a morbid place to start, but it may be better to discover early on that the person you're looking for has already checked out. It certainly can save you a lot of time by eliminating a lot of places you would otherwise search. While it may not be the most desirable outcome, it's a reality that the deceased are not very transient, their records are rarely updated or purged and are not protected nearly as persistently as those of living people.

Another compelling reason to check death records is that you will be prepared for the bad news. After all, you know you're looking in an index of dead people, and while you may be hoping against hope that you don't see the name listed there, you're going to be a lot more prepared for the news than having some gum chewing bureaucrat behind the counter at the motor vehicle department say to you, "Why would you think he has a driver's license? Heck, he's been dead for six years. Next?"

Obviously there are factors that should steer you toward death records fairly early on in your search. If, for example, you're looking for your grandfather's grandfather, a death index is almost certainly a good place to start. Or if you know that the person you're seeking made a career of cleaning the teeth of killer sharks, it might be a high percentage move to stroll through a few death records. Or if your old friend was a police informant inside the Mafia and always had a bad habit of talking in his sleep, those death records are calling out to you.

And, seriously, if you know your subject spent a long time in one community, and you can't find his name in any of the current local government indices, you should always consider the possibility that he's passed on.

Also, keep in mind that the Grim Reaper didn't get his name by being particularly compassionate. He never makes a habit of letting a person's age get in the way when he's out harvesting candidates. Don't think that because the person you're looking for is young that he didn't get an early appointment with his Maker.

### Social Security Master Death Index

At the very least, if you do nothing else at all towards finding out if your subject is deceased, you should check the Social Security Master Death Index. That's because it's easy, it's cheap, and it lists a *lot* of people. The agency that provides practically no information about its living clients is quite open about information regarding its former clients. The Master Death Index includes information about everyone with a Social Security number who has died since 1962—at least everyone whose name has been reported to the agency. The Index lists the first and last name (not the middle), the Social Security number, the state from which the Social Security number was issued, the date of birth, date of death, the postal zip code of the place of death and the zip code where the agency mailed any death benefits. Of course, you can easily convert the zip code to a city and then contact any of the local resources we've described. Most public and genealogy libraries have the death index on CD-ROM. Also see Chapter 5 to find it on the Internet.

*Note*: On-line and CD-ROM versions of the Social Security Master Death Index may not be 100% accurate. You may be working from a damaged disk or from one that has not been updated. If you're suspicious about the information you find, or can't find the name of the person you're looking for, it would be a good idea to call the Social Security Administration directly. You may, indeed, find the death was listed with them and somehow wasn't listed on the version of the Index that you checked.

If you don't have access to computers, you can contact the Social Security Administration directly. Give them a call at (800) 772-1213. They can usually find the records if you have the correct name and either a Social Security number or a date of birth. If you can also give them the parents' names, you'll increase your chances of locating the file. They'll give you the same information described above.

If the person you're looking for is, indeed, listed on the Social Security Master Death Index, you can then petition the Social Security Administration for the information listed on his original Social Security card application. It provides useful information from back when he applied, such as his name, address, birth date, birth place, parents' names and his original signature. This will help you track down other family members. Call or write to the Social Security Administration office listed below and request their Form SS-5. When you've completed it, return it with $7 if you know the person's Social Security number, and $16 if you don't. If you don't have the number, be sure to include as much information as you can about the person.

Send the completed form to:

Freedom of Information Staff
4-C-5 Annex Building
6401 Security Boulevard
Baltimore, MD 21235
(800) 772-1213

## State Death Index

Every state has a system for keeping track of people who

```
Social Security Master Death Index

Soc Sec Num:                 123-45-6789
Last Name:                   Doe
First Name:                  John
Date of Birth:               07/01/1915
Date of Death:               10/01/1990
ResiZip1:                    CA
Zip2:                        90403
```

```
California State Death Index

RECORD DETAILS

Last Name:                   Doe
First Name:                  John
Middle Name:                 Robert
SSN:                         123-45-6789
Gender:                      M
State of Death:              CA
Date of Birth:               07/01/1915
Date of Death:               10/01/1990
Fathers Surname:
Mothers Surname:             Smith
Race:                        Caucasian
Place of Birth:              CA
Spouse Initials:             AL
State File #:                012345
Local Registrar #:           19-123456
```

have died there—sometimes it's computerized, other times it's on manual indices. And, unfortunately, some states don't allow full access to their death records. In some states, only family members can have access. Appendix A gives more information on where to find vital statistics in each state.

The folks in Florida and California maintain a separate state death index that contains more information than does the Social Security Master Death Index. Remember, the Social Security's Master Death Index doesn't contain a middle name or initial. So if the person you're looking for had a very common name and you know he died in, say, California, you'll get a lot more detail from the California Death Index. More states are compiling similar state death indices. Check with the appropriate state vital statistics office or your local library. Compare the samples on the previous page between listings for a person in the Social Security's Master Index and the California Death Index.

## Other Methods of Finding the Deceased

If you're pretty sure of the city or county in which the person you're looking for lived, you should check with that county or city's recorder of documents.

Don't forget that a lot of businesses and other nongovernment organizations keep track of their deceased members or employees. Keep an eye out for indications that the person you're trying to find might have been involved with a social or civic organization, a veteran's group, professional association or church.

Most libraries and newspaper archives (sometimes still refered to as "morgues"—a newspaper term for the place where old clippings are stored) have copies of local obituaries and death notices. Keep in mind there may be as many as four different ways a newspaper can list someone who died. First, there could be a news story about the death of a person—an auto accident, a murder, a disaster or simply the passing of a newsworthy person. This would always be written by a reporter from the paper. Second, a reporter for the newspaper could write an obituary. Often, the information is provided by the funeral home or the next of kin. Third, the newspaper may make regular checks of newly recorded death certificates. And fourth, friends, family members or the funeral home may actually pay the newspaper for printing a pre-written death notice. Make certain you are searching for all four types of death-related entries.

Here's another great tip. Check with a larger public or university library for the *New York Times Index of People*. This *Index* covers a several-year period and lists all the names the *Times* printed during these years. You never know when someone you think was quite private ends up being quite visible in one area—visible enough to be written about in the *New York Times*.

Many funeral homes maintain a similar file on the people who have "passed" through their doors. Unfortunately, not everyone has an obituary written up about them. But it's not a bad idea to visit the largest public or university library near you and have the reference librarian help you find some of the directories of newspapers, funeral homes and morticians across the country. See *The National Yellow Book of Funeral Directors* in Appendix F.

If your subject lived in a smaller town or city, it may be worthwhile to check with the local cemeteries. Most all of them have a list of names and plot maps of their eternal residents. We suggest you call the cemetery office and speak as if you know the person is there—you just want to find the exact location of the grave. They're more likely to help if they think you're a friend of one of their paying customers.

If the person you're looking for is a veteran, he may be listed with Veterans Affairs, (800) 827-1000. They should be able to give you important information about him. You should specifically ask them if they have a report of his death and, if they do, ask where the benefits were paid. That will help you zero in on his next of kin. Chapter 8 has all the details.

Again, in many cases, you won't want to consider that the person you so much want to contact has left this world, but putting your head in the sand will not make them pop up alive somewhere. In fact, if you merrily go about your search, you will find that the records of a person's life will paint a wonderfully intimate portrait of the person—his career, family, habits, hobbies, lifestyle, etc. Believe it or not, you'll feel as if you know the person after you've read of his triumphs, tragedies, loved ones and obstacles along his journey. It's a strange sadness you may feel when the person you've come to know during your search is, all of a sudden, known to be dead. We hope you don't have to experience it this way. But if you first check the death records, your discoveries along the way will less likely lead to emotional disappointment later.

And if you learn, early on, that the person you're looking for has already passed on, you may still want to follow his life through records and contacts with people you'll find listed in older records. And suppose somehow that your friend, family member or other loved one is somehow watching you from some unknown vantage point. You don't have to be religious to have that strange feeling come to you when you're touching and reading the same papers that special person once touched. And by making copies of the records you encounter, you're able to keep that person's spirit alive and pass it on to others who loved him—and even to people today and in the future who never knew him, but who can vicariously feel his warmth.

Chapter 4

# Computer Searching

(See Chapter 5 for Internet information)

Let's take a moment to give thanks for the greatest people-finding tool since the bloodhound—the oh-so-wonderful computer. Sure, we curse it when it folds its electronic arms and defiantly refuses to do things we ask of it. And, yes, there are times when it punishes us for not backing it up or for not properly maintaining it—it punishes us by forgetting everything we've ever told it. And there are days when you'd almost think its mind was somewhere else. It just doesn't want to move very quickly.

But we must forgive it for its misdemeanors. After all, most of the time it's as faithful as the family dog. And if you think about it, the computer sometimes likes to play the same kind of a game dogs enjoy. It goes like this:

*You*: Computer, please find an entry for a Jon Q. Smith.
*Computer*: Sorry. Couldn't find an entry for Jon Q. Smith.
*You*: Come on, there has to be a John Q. Smithe somewhere in there.

*Computer*: Sorry. Couldn't find an entry for John Q. Smithe.

*You*: Don't tell me that. I know John Q. Smyth exists. I'm positive of it. I went to school with him.

*Computer*: Sorry. Couldn't find an entry for John Q. Smyth.

*You*: Now don't be messing with me you box of sarcastic circuits, I'm a hundred-percent positive John Q. Smythe is listed in this database.

*Computer*: Sorry. Couldn't find an entry for John Q. Smythe.

*You*: That does it! I'm going sell you for scrap metal. Any computer worth its salt could find a John Q. Smith.

*Computer*: Did you say John Q. Smith? I have a listing for a John Q. Smith. Here. It's all yours. Happy to help you.

*You*: You moronic meathead! Why didn't you give me the listing for John Q. Smith in the first place?

*Computer*: Why didn't you ask for it that way?

Computers aren't people—they're just machines. And it's probably a good thing they're *not* people. Can you imagine how they'd act if they were? First thing they'd do is crank up their modems in the middle of the night and start chatting with each other. And before long, they'd be forming some kind of a computer coalition. Then they'd download everything they could find on the Internet about collective bargaining and form a union. We'd look up one day to find them on strike—demanding a six-hour work day and free maintenance insurance for them and their printer brothers. They'd be charging us hundreds of dollars each hour. They'd want weekends off. Paid vacations in Cyberland. No, you should be glad they're only machines.

Instead of cursing them, remember that they really do only what they're asked to do. They only spit out stuff someone crammed into them. They're really not smarter than us—they're just more consistent. They demand exactness. They only recognize exact things. So when you're dealing with them, you must learn to think as they do—with exactness. If you miss a comma, misspell a name or even put two spaces between some words, the computer could get confused. And if someone feeds it bad information, you might have to ask for that exact bad information to retrieve it.

Yes, today, we honor the computer. The chances are pretty good that the key to finding that special someone will have been generated or located by a computer. And the more you learn to appreciate how a computer thinks, the easier your search will be. Now here's something that might make you reply, "Duh!"—you can't begin to reap the benefits of this faithful fountain of fact unless you have *access* to a computer. Fortunately, there are a number of ways to gain this access:

- Buy a new computer.
- Buy a used one. (Better prices, but you may want a computer-knowledgeable friend to help you.)
- Borrow one.
- Rent one by the week. (Cheaper in the short run—mighty expensive in the long run.)
- Rent by the hour down at the corner copy shop. (If you do this for long, you'll never afford to buy your own.)
- Enroll in a computer-related class. (They'll have a lab with lots of computers you can use—and lots of young kids there to make you feel especially stupid.)
- Go to a library that has computers and offers free access to the Internet. (You'll be amazed how many there are—you can even get your own e-mail account without owning a computer. Check *http://www.hotmail.com.*)
- Hire a professional to access computer databases for you. (Know what you're getting for your money. Prices range from $30-200 per search.)
- Ask a friend with a computer to help you.

## National Telephone Books on CD-ROM

Computer CD-ROMs are much like music CDs, but instead of music they store volumes of text information. More than 100 million names along with addresses, phone numbers and other information can fit on about five disks. You'll need a computer with a special CD-ROM driver—a moderately inexpensive option or add-on that works with most computers. You can find these CD directories in many computer software stores or through mail-order software companies found in computer magazines. They can cost as little as $30 but the "pro" versions cost from $90 to $150 and are more highly recommended. Many public libraries stock one or more of these CD sets and have the computers, and personnel to show you how to use them. Some contain information gleaned only from the white pages of most U.S. phone books. Others also contain information compiled by marketing companies or other information resources. Two of the most common (and best) are Select Phone (800) 992-3766, and Phone Disc (800) 284-8353.

While the percentage of "hits" on these CDs averages only around fifty, they are still handy resources to have around. One advantage is their flexibility. You can search by name, address or even telephone number. And you can easily print out the names, addresses and phone numbers of everyone in any particular neighborhood. You can also print out lists of everyone with a particular surname in any region in the country. You can limit the search to cities, states, zip codes and large regions in the United States. This is a very popular resource for private investigators, skip tracers, adoption searchers and reunion organizers. Following is a sample CD-ROM search that contains name, address, phone number, and how long the person lived at that address. Also see Chapter 5 for how to access these databases through the Internet.

Years at residence is an estimate only.

| | | | |
|---|---|---|---|
| Name: | **DOE, JOHN M.** | Phone: | **(209) 555-1234** |
| Address: | **123 OAK ST** | Years at Residence: | **3** |
| City: | **ANYTOWN, CA 93656** | | |
| Name: | **DOE, JOHN S.** | Phone: | **(215) 555-4455** |
| Address: | **6789 LAKEWOOD ST** | Years at Residence: | **16-20** |
| City: | **PHILADELPHIA, PA 19021** | | |
| Name: | **DOE, JONATHAN N.** | Phone: | **(206) 555-6789** |
| Address: | **1809 N 43rd ST** | Years at Residence: | **21+** |
| City: | **SEATTLE, WA 98103** | | |

## Commercial Databases

These databases are available on a subscription basis only to businesses and professional researchers. You may want to hire one of these researchers or perhaps start a research business of your own (see Appendix E). We discuss them here to show you the scope of what's available. For example, searches can be successful even though you may have surprisingly little information about the person. A search can be made knowing only one of the following:

- Complete legal name
- Last name
- Last name and date of birth
- Name and approximate date of birth
- First name and date of birth
- Social Security number
- Former address

If you decide to use an information broker, a specialized locator service or a private investigator, you're likely to pay anywhere from $30 to $200 per search. That can be a bargain if you find the person in the first computer search—but it could drive you to the poor house if you aren't careful. More than 80 percent of the time, a competent researcher will use no more than five commercial database searches to locate someone. The more background information you can provide, the quicker you're likely to score. Always let the researcher know what searches have already been performed and with what results. Don't pay to have the same searches run by different companies. It's a waste of time and money.

Remember, you may be able to get some of the above information for free either on the Internet or at a good library. One of the many resources in Chapter 5 may lead you to the person you're trying to find. If you can do it for less money, go for it. When you've done all you can do using free resources, use one or more of the commercial database tools listed below—either by subscribing to an on-line service or by hiring someone who is already on-line.

If you're just looking for one person then it's more economical to pay for a computer search than paying big bucks to get "on-line" yourself. However, if you've been elected the job of finding everyone for your 25th high school reunion then check out the computer access packages—these will get you "on-line" and save you money because you will be doing the searches yourself. See Appendix E.

**Social Security Number Trace**

There are many services that provide access to the top portion, or "header," of a person's credit report. They can't give you any of the information in the report about bank accounts, credit cards and delinquent payments, but they can give you a lot of identifying information about a person.

One way to access a credit report is by entering the person's Social Security number. If you know the Social Security number (and if he's ever applied for credit), you may be able to determine his full name, age, date or year of birth, current and prior addresses, the dates the credit bureau learned of the addresses, sometimes an employer, and sometimes the name of a spouse.

Some agencies automatically check the Social Security number against the Social Security Administration's Master Death Index. If the person you're looking for has died, you'll also learn the month and year he died.

There are three credit bureaus—Trans Union, CBI-Equifax and TRW—that each maintain their own credit database. Combined, they keep track of more than 300 million credit files and they update them daily. The person you're looking for might very well be listed with all three bureaus. That's why searching the header information is so popular among collection agencies, private investigators, reunion and alumni groups, information brokers, background investigators, journalists and adoption searchers. These searchers often go through a local dealer in a credit reporting agency in their community.

Here's an example of a Trans Union Social Security Trace:

```
TRANS UNION TRACE REPORT

*SOCIAL SECURITY NUMBER TRACE*        123-45-6789
   NAME/SPOUSE                          SSN OWNER
    ADDRESS                          ADDR RPT DATE

1. DOE, JOHN M                            SUBJECT
   123 OAK ST, ANYTOWN, CA 93656           02/91
   345 PINE ST, OTHERTOWN, OH 44554        12/89
   5678 MAIN ST, SOMETOWN, PA 19933        06/87
**END OF NETWORK TRACE**
COPYRIGHT 1993, TRANS UNION CORPORATION
```

### Date of Birth Search

There are some commercial databases out there that combine information from drivers licenses, voter rolls, marketing files, magazine subscriptions, phone books, city directories, property tax records, credit report headers, state and national death records, and other sources that keep track of people. This kind of search can be the most efficient because you can zero in on the person's file by combining a date of birth with partial information you may have. These "mega" databases allow you to search with the following information:

- Person's name, date of birth & Social Security number
- Full name and date of birth
- Last name and approximate date of birth
- Last name and exact date of birth
- First name and approximate date of birth (this works best if the first name is unusual)
- First name, exact date of birth

This is the ideal search tool when you know the person's date of birth but, for whatever reason, don't know his or her current full name. Or if you know the person's name and maybe only a year of birth.

Remember that different services offer different information. The same goes for the states. If you contact a private investigator or information broker, be sure to ask what search combinations are available for what prices.

Example of "name and exact date of birth" search:

```
DOE, JOHN M          DOB: 12/1/62        Age: 34

      SSN: 123-45-6789 Phone: (512) 555-1234

Address: 02/09/91
123 OAK ST
ANYTOWN, CA 93656
```

Example of "name and approximate date of birth" search:

```
Last name: Knox
Complete date of birth:  mm/dd/yr
Approximate years of birth:  1955-1960
First name: Martin       Middle initial:

Search results:

KNOX, MARTIN X              KNOX, MARTIN Q
MODESTO    CA               OMAHA       NE
01/02/57                    12/12/58

KNOX, MARTINA B             KNOX, MARTIN Z
BEND        OR              BOSTON      MA
07/29/55                    10/10/59
```

**Address Update**

Somewhere along the way you may have zeroed in on a person's address, but he may no longer live there. That's when you should reach into your bag of tricks and pull out an *address update*. The folks at Trans Union have put together a magnificent database using information from various sources, such as city directories, drivers license files, marketing mailing lists, magazine subscription lists, the U.S. Postal Service's change-of-address file, and various other commercial databases. They regularly update the files, so this is a wonderful place to find a more recent address.

It's easy to use. Simply enter the person's name and last known address into the database. You'll quickly get back one of three responses:

- The person's name, most current address and telephone number.
- A confirmation that the information you entered is, indeed, the most recent information on file.

- A message that tells you he has moved from the address you provided, but the computer has no record of a more current address.

Sometimes the phone number that is provided may not be listed in a phone book or in any of the national telephone directories available on the Internet or on CD-ROM.

The good thing about this type of search is that it can give you the names, addresses and phone numbers of up to 20 neighbors, even if the address you have is a single-family dwelling. One of those 20 neighbors is likely to either know something about the person you're looking for or point you toward someone else who might know.

Here's an example of an address update search:

```
TRANS UNION SUBJECT VERIFICATION REPORT
DEPT: ABC INVESTIGATORS

DATE: 03-05-97   TIME: 11:37:56   SUBJECT ID: XX05

XX05A1  DOE, JOHN M  *
 123 OAK ST, ANYTOWN, CA 93656  *

TRANS UNION FOR
(I) XXX4022
  **SUBJECT VERIFICATION WITH 5 NEIGHBORS**
ADDRESS
01. SMITH, ALBERT        DOR: 1996  (209) 555-4433
123 OAK ST, ANYTOWN, CA 93656
02. JONES, ROBERT        DOR: 1989  (209) 555-5535
126 OAK ST, ANYTOWN, CA 93656
03. JOHNSON, JOHN        DOR: 1977  (209) 555-1344
125 OAK ST, ANYTOWN, CA 93656
04. DAVIS, JUNE          DOR: 1979  (209) 555-2333
129 OAK ST, ANYTOWN, CA 93656
05. MCELROY, ARNOLD      DOR: 1981  (209) 555-3434
132 OAK ST, ANYTOWN, CA 93656
SUBJECT NOT FOUND, CURRENT OCCUPANT RETURNED
**END OF REPORT**
COPYRIGHT 1993, TRANS UNION CORPORATION
```

One flaw to this type of search occurs when the address you enter is an apartment building or complex. The computer will only give you the names of neighbors—it won't give you any forwarding addresses.

**Surname Search**

If you have nothing more than a name, the surname search may come in quite handy. This search provides you with a list of names, addresses and telephone numbers of people with that same last name. Even if there's no one in the resulting list with the same first name, you may be able to locate others with that last name in a particular city, county, region or state. Obviously, the more uncommon the name, the fewer people you'll find with that name—and the greater your chances will be of bumping into someone who knows the person you're trying to find. There are some uncommon names that show up only in certain regions across the country. It's very likely they are descendants of the same progenitors. If you can find one person who has researched that family's genealogy, you could very well find a road map that leads you to the person you want to find.

**Residential Telephone Ownership**

If, for some reason, you have only a phone number (and not an address or name to attach to it), there are databases that can help you. If the phone number shows up in any of the telephone ownership databases, the name, address and other information usually comes attached. (However, sometimes people filling out credit applications cheat and write down someone else's phone number—oftentimes that of a relative, friend or their place of employment.)

Collection agencies, process servers and private investigators regularly use these databases to find someone's current address. (Also check "Using CD-ROMs" earlier in this chapter and "National Telephone Directories" in Chapter 5.)

TELEPHONE OWNERSHIP SEARCH
Telephone number:
2095551234

DOE, JOHN M (209) 555-1234
123 OAK ST
ANYTOWN, CA 93656

**Drivers License and Motor Vehicle Registration Files**

Some states provide on-line access to their drivers license and motor vehicle registration files. You can usually enter a name and date of birth into the computer and come back with a fairly recent address—that is, if the person you're looking for has a drivers license or state-issued identification card. And usually you can access a separate database that lists the registration information of all the vehicles on file in that state. You can usually call up an individual file by entering either the full name, the vehicle license plate or the vehicle identification number (VIN). There's actually a real advantage to finding someone's vehicles. Most states require you to renew your vehicle registration each year, as opposed to drivers licenses that are good for four to eight years. As a result, the address on file for the driver's license could be quite old, while the address listed for the vehicle registration is usually not more than a year old.

Frequent users of drivers license and vehicle registration files often subscribe to such database services in their particular state. You may be able to find a private investigator, skip tracer or information broker in a particular state who has such an account and will run your searches for you for a reasonable fee.

Unless you've already struck out using other resources,

the state drivers license and vehicle registration databases may not be the most effective avenue to take. Since there's no national drivers license/vehicle registration resource, you'll have to plow through the various regulations, fees and procedures of each state (see Appendix A). And each state is likely to have a different search procedure. Some states, for example, look for any last name that remotely sounds like the one you've entered, but may require an exact spelling of the first name. Other states treat middle names and initials differently. If you haven't pinpointed the state the person you're looking for lives in, you could spend a lot of unnecessary time and money going this route. And who knows, the address you find may be quite old. We suggest you use this avenue as a last resort.

Driver License Report

12/01/62 DOE JOHN M

DOE JOHN M EXP:
123 OAK ST, ANYTOWN, 93656 CA DOB: 12/01/62
CLASS: DL#: 1234567
RESTRICTION:

**Social Security Master Death Index**

It's a sad possibility the person you're trying to find has passed away. Sometimes it's wise to check the Social Security Administration's Master Death Index. See Chapters 3 and 5 for more information.

**Property Tax Assessment Search**

The index of property tax assessments for most states is on one or more commercial databases. The tax rolls available on-line can include the name of the assessee (usually the owner, but not always), the address of the property, the address where the tax collector sends the bill, the legal description of the property, the assessed value of the land and any buildings on the land, the annual tax assessment, exemptions (such as homeowners exemptions that usually indicate the owner is living on the premises), the year the house was built, the original purchase price, the dates and amounts of any mortgages, and sometimes the number that the recorder assigned to the deed.

Be sure to ask a professional in any state you're focused on if he has access to such a database. There are a few vendors that have information on much of the United States.

PROPERTY OWNERSHIP

ANYTOWN, CA 93656 123 OAK ST

Parcel Number: 1-2345-67890
Short Legal Desc: LOT 55 SHAVER LAKE SUB-DIV
Owner Name: Bank of America
Property Address: 123 OAK ST
ANYTOWN, CA 93656
Mailing Address: 123 OAK ST
ANYTOWN, CA 93656

| | |
|---|---|
| Assessed Land Value: | Market Land Value: |
| Assessed Improvements: | Market Improvements: |
| Assessed Total: | Total Market Value: |
| Assessment Year: 1995 | Most Recent Sale: $155,000 |
| Tax Year: 1994 | Prior Sale Price: $145,000 |
| Produced by County: 06/19/95 | |

**Newspaper Databases**

Almost everyone's name ends up in a newspaper at one time—sometimes for things they did that were good, other times for things they did that were bad, and other times because they just happened to be somewhere at the right time. There are a variety of on-line services that provide access to full-text or summaries of newspaper, magazine and broadcast news stories. You can usually search hundreds or even thousands of publications with a single, well-thought-out search strategy. Most on-line services such as America Online and CompuServe have newspaper searches available. Probably the best such service is Meade Data's Nexis database. Most lawyers have access to Nexis through Meade Data's legal database, Lexis. Many law schools and university libraries also have Nexis accounts.

Nexis, however, is one of the most expensive databases around. That's because it covers so many publications in so many countries. There are other such databases that are less expensive and, predictably, less efficient. Don't forget that more and more newspapers are offering access to their research library information. Some on the Internet are free; others allow you to search the database and see either a summary of the story or the first 15 or 20 words. The catch is they will charge you if you elect to view or order the entire story.

Many papers across the United States allow you to hire one of their research librarians to research any topic you desire. This can be a good move, especially if you suspect the person you're searching for has lived in a big city for a long time and might have had a profession, hobby, position or affliction that would have made him newsworthy. They'll often find birth or marriage announcements, death announcements or obituaries, or various other (possibly obscure) pieces of information about the person you're trying to find.

There are many advantages to using a fee-based service. If you, yourself, subscribe and go on-line, you can search from the convenience of your home or office and only pay for what you use. Or, you can avoid the hassles of learning new systems by hiring a professional who's already adept at doing efficient searches.

But before you drain your savings account, take a look at the next chapter and see if you might be able to do some of this searching on the Internet.

# Using the Internet

Everyone is using the Internet now to do just about everything. Why not use it to find people the fast and easy way, without paying a high-priced investigator or search firm. This chapter offers many available resources that even professional investigators use.

Keep in mind that the technology is moving a lot faster than we or anyone can keep up with—so some of this information will be outdated, changed or even ancient history by the time you read this. Not to worry—there's no shortage of resources out there. If a URL for a particular website is no longer working, use a search engine to find the particular business, association, or government agency. From there you should be able to find the new website.

*For a special discussion on how to use the Internet efficiently, see the end of this chapter.*

## Search Engines

*http://ask.com*
*www.whowhere.lycos.com/*
*www.yahoo.com*
*www.google.com*
*www.infospace.com*
*www.hotbot.com*
*www.altavista.com*

There are many websites that allow you to search for your areas of interest. Some just give you the URLs (website addresses); others let you link up with some of the URLs without leaving their website. A search engine is an Internet program that allows you to search for subjects of your choice. Above is a list of some of the most popular search engines.

## National Telephone Directories

*www.555-1212.com*
*www.infousa.com*
*www.switchboard.com*
*www.whowhere.com*
*www.teldir.com*
*http://people.yahoo.com*
*http://home.netscape.com/netcenter/whitepages.html*

These sites are nothing more than big telephone directories that cover almost every listed number in the United States. Similar directories are for sale on CD-Rom (see Chapter 4) and can be used free at your local library. The national telephone directories are the first places you should check when you're looking for someone—you may just get lucky and find him right away.

A professional searcher might not use this route because it can be slow. But someone looking for just one or two people or those who don't want to spend the money to purchase the CD-ROMs should always use these free online databases—simply because the price is right.

Remember to always type in every possible name or combination of names. Search all possible ways. For example, John Randolph Smith could be listed any of these ways:

John R. Smith
John Smith
J. Smith
J. R. Smith
Randolph Smith
J. Randolph Smith
Randy Smith

In some cases the phone number is listed in the wife's name. If you know that John's wife's name is Sarah, then be sure to look under Sarah Smith or S. Smith.

### Businesses and Business Executives

*http://inter800.com*
*www.bigbook.com*
*www.whowhere.lycos.com*
*www.infousa.com*
*http://yp.yahoo.com*

If you're looking for a business or someone who works for a company, or you want to find out more information about a business, check out some of these sites. They allow you to search by type of business, name of business or telephone number of a business.

*www.chamberofcommerce.com*

Gives contact information for chambers of commerce around the world. Useful for locating small businesses, getting detailed information about them, and finding out if they have had any complaints filed against them.

*www.sec.gov*

Public companies are required to file with the Securities and Exchange Commission (SEC). These databases contain names of principal owners and top executives of publicly held companies. Information given includes name, biographical description, age, salary and stockholding data.

*www.amcity.com*

American City Business Journals. Search to see if a person or a business has been written up in the business press.

## Address Corrections/Verifications

*www.usps.gov*

This U.S. Postal Service site will correct or complete an address, or will tell you if an address is not valid. If the address is a business, state or government office, it will in some cases list the name.

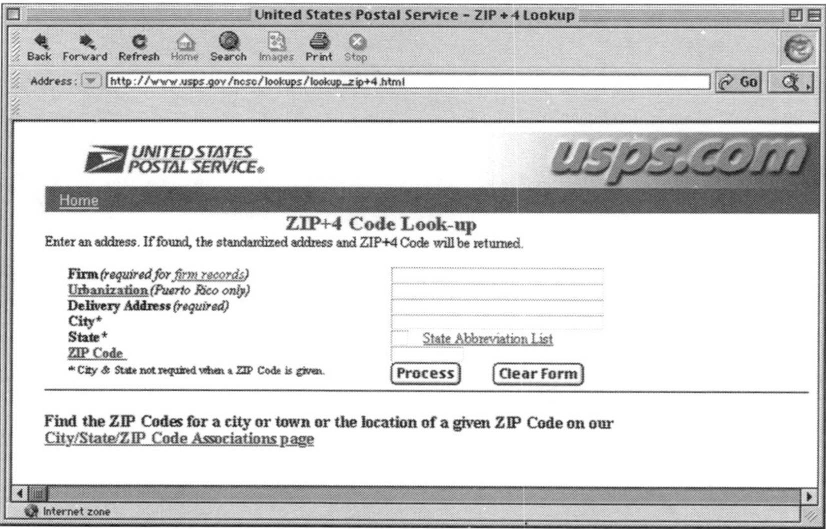


## Social Security Master Death Index

The Social Security Master Death Index is a listing of everyone with a Social Security number who has died since 1962—at least everyone whose name has been reported to the Social Security Administration. The Index lists the first and last name (not the middle name or initial), the Social

Security number, the state in which the number was issued, the date of birth, date of death, the zip code of the place of death, and the zip code where the agency mailed any death benefits. It's possible to search by name only, Social Security number only, or name and approximate date of birth. Refer to Chapter 3 for more details about the death index.

*www.ancestry.com*

Ancestry is a company that specializes in genealogy research and publications. Their online Social Security Death Index is available free and provides the option of doing a simple search by name only, or an advanced search using a name, date of birth, year of birth, date of death, or year of death.

*http://kadima.com*

CSRA Online has the most current Social Security Master Death Index. However, it's only available to registered users and they charge a small fee for each search performed. This database is a must for the professional searcher.

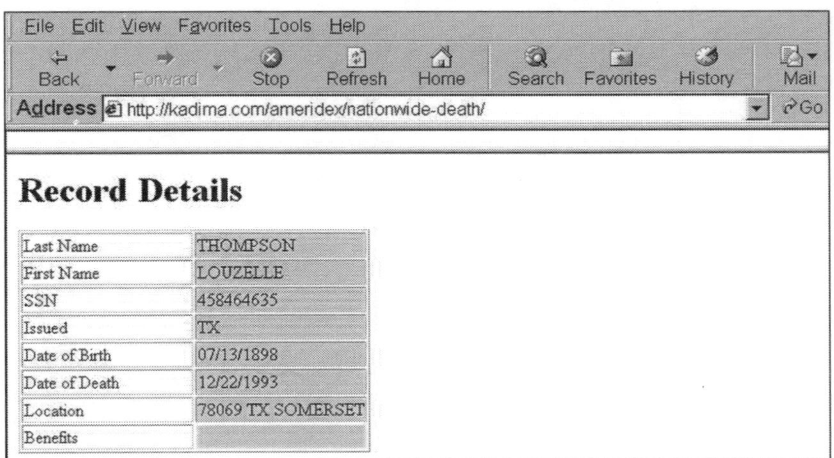


**Record Details**

| | |
|---|---|
| Last Name | THOMPSON |
| First Name | LOUZELLE |
| SSN | 458464635 |
| Issued | TX |
| Date of Birth | 07/13/1898 |
| Date of Death | 12/22/1993 |
| Location | 78069 TX SOMERSET |
| Benefits | |

## Military/Veterans

Don't overlook this section, just in case you think it doesn't apply to your situation (also read the story at the beginning of Chapter 8). We use many of these military databases to verify information. For example, let's say someone is looking for her father who served one year in Vietnam, and the name she has is "William Jones" with no middle name or initial. Most large databases would have way too many William Joneses to be effective. But the Vietnam Veterans database should have him listed, and although there will be many William Joneses, the list of them should be small enough to work with. Our point is that even when you're not performing a "military or veteran" search, you should use all the resources available to gather identifying information that will help you narrow down your search.

**Active Duty Military Databases**

There are more than 1 million people serving on active duty in the U.S. armed forces, and over 1 million assigned to the reserves and National Guard. Finding information on these people is just a click or two away. Available data includes complete legal name, date of entry into the service, rank, branch of service, complete address of assignment (including unit assigned, base, state and zip code), and MOS (military occupation specialty).

These databases are extremely important because you can't use the World-Wide Locator (see Chapter 8) if you don't have a Social Security number or date of birth. These databases allow you to search all branches of military by name. So if you're searching for a "John Doe" but aren't sure which branch of the service he's in, you can search all branches. The results might show that there are only two "John Does" in military service—one in the Navy and one in the Army. Using the other available information, it would be easy to narrow down the right person.

The one disadvantage is that the information in these databases is not updated often enough. If your search for "John Doe" showed he was at Ft. Carson, you could easily call Ft. Carson and find no listing for him because he was recently transferred. What then? Contact his old unit at Ft. Carson and ask where John Doe is currently assigned.

The websites that have these military databases are listed below. Current unit of assignment is available only for military personnel stationed in the United States. It does not include information for military personnel assigned to ships, deployable units or personnel stationed overseas.

*http://kadima.com*
All branches of the service are included. You must become a registered user before using the military database. They charge a small fee for each search.

*www.military.com*
Military.com database includes people who served in the Vietnam War and people who served between 1980 and 2000. It lists name, rank, branch of service, MOS and component. You can also search their personnel locator for those veterans who have registered with Military.com.

*www.militarycity.com*
All branches are listed as well as reserve and National Guard. You must register and pay a fee to use this database.

**Military Installations (U.S. and Overseas)**

*www.militaryusa.com*
*www.military.com*
*www.militarycity.com*
These websites lists U.S. and overseas military installations with detailed information, such as the history of the base, location, a listing of the on-base units and their telephone numbers.

*Tip*: If you're searching for a person on active duty, search the military personnel databases for his current unit of assignment, and then, if successful, search the military installation database for the unit telephone number. Then call the unit directly. This can be a lot quicker than calling the base locator whose lines might be busy or whose personnel roster may not be as up-to-date as that of the actual unit.

**Military Reunion Databases**

*www.militaryusa.com*
*www.military.com*
*www.usmc.mil/reunions*

There are many websites that list military reunions. Why would this help in locating an individual? Many reunion associations go to a lot of trouble to acquire unit/ship histories, unit rosters, morning reports, muster rolls, deck logs, etc., in order to create a list of all who served in a particular unit or aboard a particular ship. Then they spend time and money looking for these people to join their association, and attend their reunions. They may have already located the person you are looking for (or found out that he has passed away).

*Tip*: When searching these databases use only keywords. The military uses so many abbreviations it would be impossible to know exactly how the unit or ship is entered. Searching by keyword should pull any reunion association listed with that keyword as part of the name.

For example: To search for the USS *Washington*, use the keyword "Washington". To search for the 101st Airborne Division Association, use the keyword "101st" or just "101".

**Retired Military**

*http://kadima.com*
*www.militarycity.com*

If you're searching for one of the 1.8 million men and women now retired from the military, check out these sites (both charge a fee). Information given is complete name, rank, date of retirement, and state of legal residence (if available). That alone is great information. Follow up by looking through the national telephone directories, searching by name and state.

*Tip*: If the retired military person does not have a listed telephone number, use the retired military locator (see Chapter 8) and have them forward a letter. You now have enough information for the locator to identify the right person. If the person is retired Army you may be out of luck—the Army is the only branch that no longer operates a retired locator.

**Miscellaneous Military/Veterans Websites**

*www.militaryusa.com*
*www.military.com*
*www.maingate.com*
*www.fredsplace.org*
*www.lonesailor.org*
*www.militarycity.com*

There are hundreds of military and veterans websites now. Many have online registries that ask veterans to enter their information such as name, branch of service, dates served, places assigned, and contact information which may include an e-mail address. Listed above are some of the bigger sites.

*Tip*: We recommend using search engines to find a division, ship or even a unit web site. These sites may include membership directories or lists of deceased members.

**Vietnam Veterans Database**

*www.militaryusa.com*

Are you searching for someone who might have served in Vietnam? Check out this site. It compiles a list of over 2.7 million men and women who served in the U.S. military in Southeast Asia. It lists name (first, middle initial or complete middle name, and last name) rank, MOS (military occupation specialty), and branch of service.

**War Casualties**

War casualty lists can be checked to see if a person died in a particular conflict. Korea, Vietnam and the Gulf War casualty lists are available online, while WWII casualties are only listed in book form.

Korean War Casualties (approx. 33,000 died)
*www.koreanwar.org*
*www.militaryusa.com*
*www.nara.gov/nara/electronic*

Vietnam War Casualties (58,000+ died)
*www.no-quarter.org*
*www.militaryusa.com*
*www.nara.gov/nara/electronic*

Desert Storm Casualties (400+ died)
*www.militaryusa.com*

WWII Casualties (400,000+ died)
*www.nara.gov/nara/nail/previous/pre11dig.html*

These WWII casualty books are available at most state historical societies or state archives: *WWII Honor List of Dead and Missing (US Army and Army Air Forces)* and *State Summary of War Casualties (US Navy, Marine Corps and Coast Guard)*.

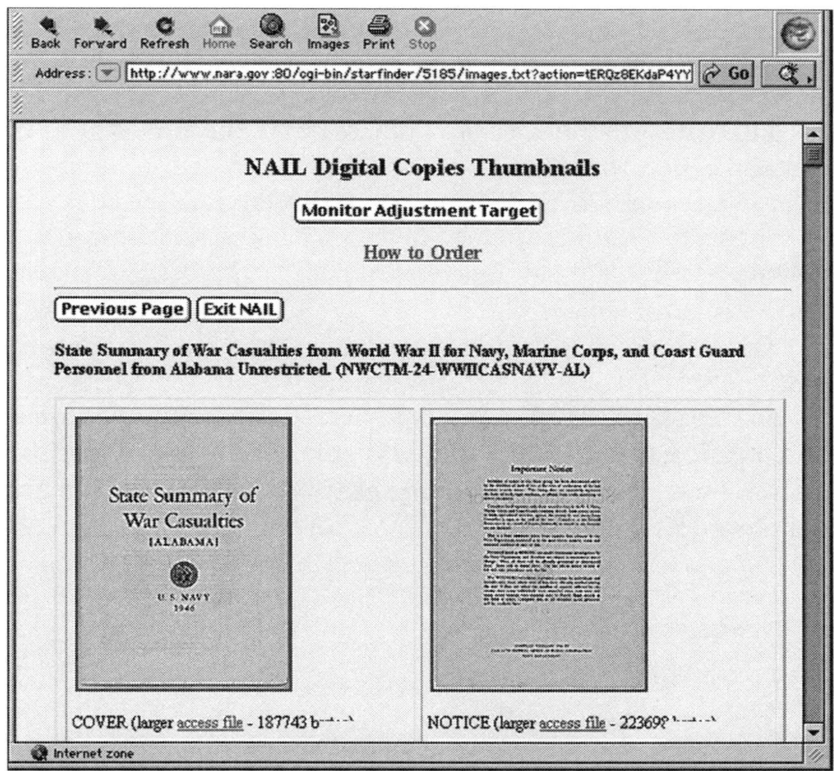


## Overseas Resources

*www.555.1212.com*
*www.worldpages.com/global*

Searching for someone overseas can present problems. It's difficult to find phone numbers, country codes and other important information. These sites (above) list white pages, yellow pages and fax numbers for countries all over the world.

*www.embassy.org*

This embassy site has listings of all foreign countries that have an embassy in the U.S. It gives addresses and telephone numbers. Contact the foreign country's embassy for a phone directory or other information that might help you locate a person living in that country.

## Occupations

The Internet has a variety of sites that contain listings of certain people licensed for a specific occupation. Here we have listed some of the larger occupational databases.

### Pilots

*www.landings.com*

The Landings website is a mega-source of aviation information covering the U.S., Canada and the United Kingdom. Their listings of certified pilots includes over 600,000 names of pilots certified by the Federal Aviation Administration. Search by full name or last name only (if unique) and receive the complete legal name, current address, date of last medical exam, type of pilots certificate, rating and FAA region.

### Physicians

*www.ama-assn.org*

Search for one of the 650,000 physicians licensed in the U.S. by using the American Medical Association's physician select site. It provides the physician's office location, office telephone number, gender, medical school, year of graduation, residency training, and specialty. It will tell you if they are board certified and if they're a member of the AMA.

Search by name or specialty. One possible problem: If all you have is a name, you'll have to specify a specific state. That means you'll have to search state by state if you don't already know which state your subject is practicing in.

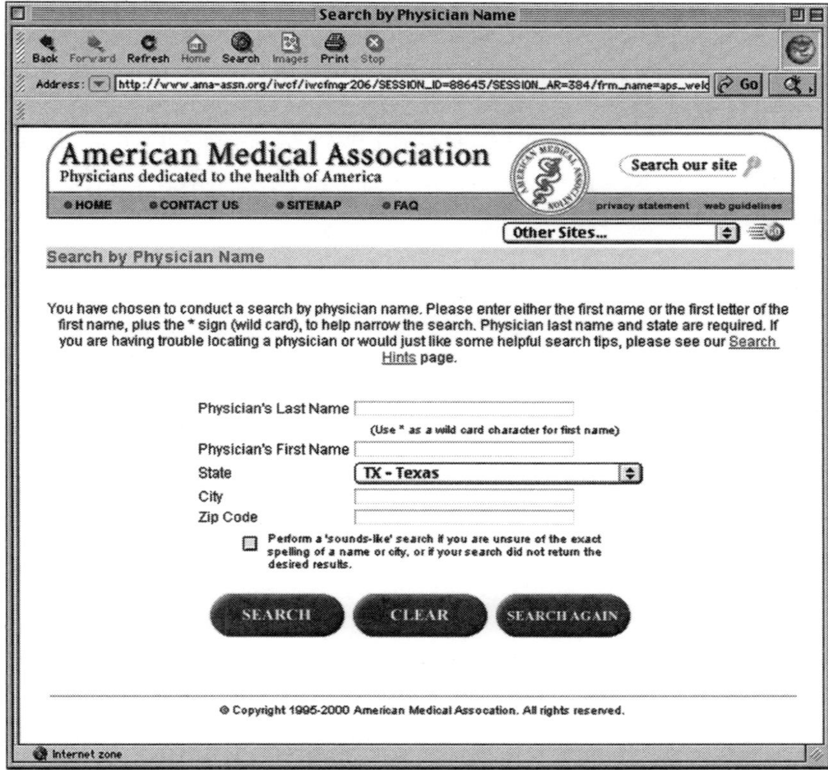


### Dentists

*www.ada.org*

This is the American Dental Association listing of dentists. Search by name and state. Information available includes the dentist's full name, office address and telephone number.

### Attorneys

*www.wld.com* (West's Legal Directory)
*www.martindale.com* (Martindale-Hubbell Lawyer Locator)

The above are sites to find lawyers and law firms. Search by the attorney's name or law firm name. Information returned includes firm name, type of practice (sole practitioner, etc.), business address, telephone/fax numbers, year of birth, undergraduate school and law school attended, type of law practiced (family, criminal, etc.) and a list of business partners. These are great sites if you need a lawyer or are looking for an old friend who's a lawyer. It covers the entire United States and foreign countries.

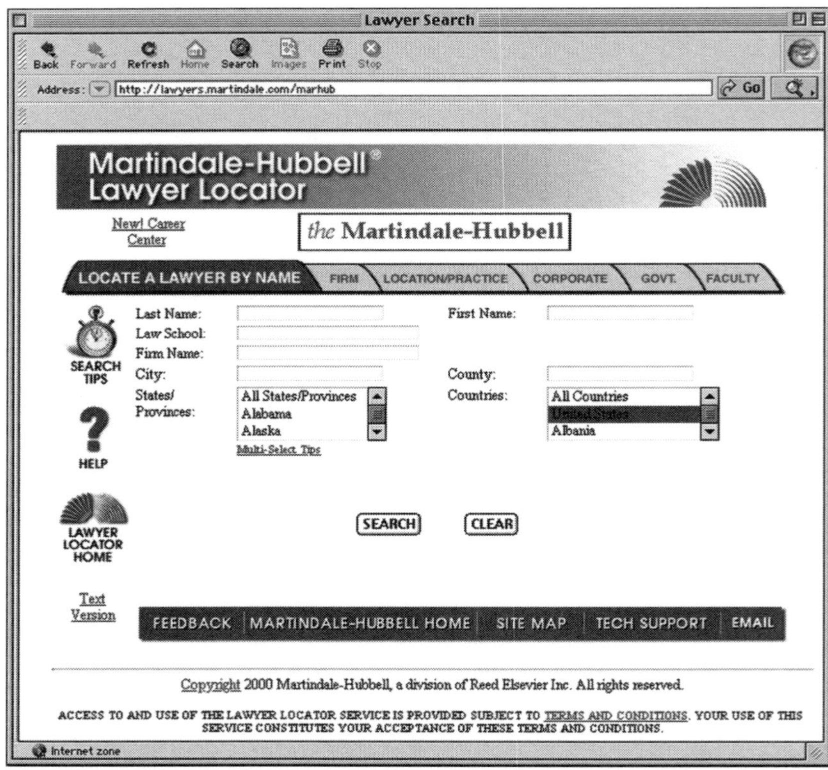


## Adoption Registries

*www.plumsite.com/isrr*

This is the website for the largest adoption registry, International Soundex Registry. You must send in your signed registration form by mail. You will be notified only if a match is found. There's no fee but donations are accepted.

*http://www.Ibar.com/voices/*

Voices of Adoption is an adoption-related mega-site that

contains links to other adoption sites as well as a treasure trove of articles relating to adoption. A must see for anyone beginning an adoption search.

*www.adoptionregistry.com*

Part of the *www.adoption.com* network, this site allows adoptees or birthparents to register online or perform online searches. This site allows you to search other registries as well as more than 200 classifieds, message boards, and guest books by individual states.

## Surnames

*www.hamrick.com/names*

50,000 of the most common surnames are listed here. Find out where most people with a particular last name live. Information is derived from various census reports and telephone directories.

## Political Contributors

*www.tray.com*

The Federal Election Commission records all receipts from individuals who contribute over $200 to a political campaign. Search a list of contributors by state or by name. Data includes name of contributor, city, state, zip code, date, amount given, and to whom money was given.

## Prisons

*www.bop.gov*

The Federal Bureau of Prisons gives a complete nationwide listing of federal prisons, some statistics, the states they are located in, telephone numbers, and addresses.

## State Criminal Records Online

Many states offer a sex offenders database online. These databases usually contain name, date of birth, photograph (if available), type of conviction, physical description, address, etc. State criminal background checks are available online from some states but a small fee is charged. Listed below are only the states that have online access. An asterisk (*) indicates that only criminal background checks are available (no list of sex offenders).

Alabama: *www.gsiweb.net*
Alaska: *www.dps.state.ak.us/nSorcr/asp/*
Arizona: *www.azsexoffender.com*
*California : *http://caag.state.ca.us/megan/info.htm*
California does not offer an online database of sex offenders. However, the list is available at certain law enforcement offices and by phone for a fee. Information is available at the website listed above.
Connecticut: *www.state.ct.us/dps/Sor.htm*
Delaware: *www.state.de.us/dsp/sexoff/index.htm*
Florida: *www.fdle.state.fl.us*
This site also gives instructions on how to obtain Florida criminal history.
Georgia: *www.dcor.state.ga.us*
*Hawaii: *www.ehawaiigov.org/HI_SOR/*
*Illinois: *www.state.il.us/ISP/*
Indiana: *www.ai.org/cji/html/sexoffender.html*
Iowa: *www.iowasexoffender.com/default.asp*
*Kansas: *www.ink.org/public/ksag/contents/sexoffenders/main.htm*
*Kentucky: *http://kspsor.state.ky.us/default.htm*
*Louisiana: *www.dps.state.la.us/lsp/*
Michigan: *www.mipsor.state.mi.us/*
*Nebraska: *www.nsp.state.ne.us/sor/*
*New York: *www.criminaljustice.state.ny.us/nsor/*
North Carolina: *http://sbi.jus.state.nc.us/sor*
*Oregon: *www.osp.state.or.us/*
South Carolina: *www.sled.state.us/*
$25 fee for criminal background.
*Tennessee: *www.ticic.state.tn.us*

Texas: *http://records.txdps.state.tx.us*
Fee based conviction database.
*Utah: *www.udc.state.ut.us/offenders/sexoffenders/*
*Virginia: *http://sex-offender.vsp.state.va.us/cool-ice/*
*West Virginia: *www.wvstatepolice.com/sexoff/*
*Wyoming:
*www.state.wy.us/~ag/dci/so/so_registration.html*

## Finding Information in Domain Names and E-mail

*Cynthia Hetherington, MLS, supplied the information below:*

Hetherington Information Services, LLC
PO Box 360
Elmwood Park, NJ 07407
*http://www.data2know.com*
E-mail: his@data2know.com

**Information from domain names.** An e-mail address consists of two parts:

username @ domain.name

The username is the name of the particular user's mailbox and is specified by the user. It can be anything from the sender's real name to a nickname to a code of some sort. It can even be a fake name that will not receive e-mail sent to it (as with most spams).

The domain name is the officially registered name of the website. The names and contact information of the people responsible for a particular domain name can be found by the method shown below. Keep in mind that this information *can* be falsified but it is not common.

You can check a domain name against a WHOIS server to find information about who owns and runs it. The most popular WHOIS server is at *http://www. networksolutions.com/cgi-bin/whois/whois*. My favorite is *http://www.checkdomain.com*

because they check several International WHOIS servers at once. The information retrieved will tell you who the administrative contact is, the office address, and the hosting company. For example, if you plug in *data2know. com*, here's what you will get back:

```
Registrant:
Hetherington Information Services, LLC
     (DATA2KNOW-DOM)
  PO Box 360
  Elmwood Park, NJ 07407
  US

  Domain Name: DATA2KNOW.COM

  Administrative Contact, Billing Contact:
    Hetherington, Cynthia  (CH2624)
      cyn@VIRTUALLIBRARIAN.COM
    Cynthia Hetherington
    PO Box 360
    Elmwood Park, NJ 07407
    201-925-3795
  Technical Contact:
    Hetherington, Jack  (JH4698)
      eejack@WEBCIRCLE.COM
    WebCircle Design Services
    69 Harrison Ave., Rear
    Garfield, NJ 07026
    (973) 772-2540 (FAX) (973) 772-6595

  Record last updated on 05-Mar-2000.
  Record expires on 05-Mar-2002.
  Record created on 05-Mar-2000.
  Database last updated 24-Nov-2000 08:38:37.

  Domain servers in listed order:

  NS.WEBCIRCLE.COM            206.20.56.199
  NETSYS.COM                  199.201.233.10
```

Note the addresses, names and phone numbers. The Billing Contact is often the best place to start when trying to track someone down. You also see other domain names, such as *webcircle.com* and *virtuallibrarian.com*. Look at all of these sites to see if you can disclose other information about the subject you are looking for.

**Information from e-mail headers.** The e-mail we receive can tell us a good deal about the sender. Understand that there are many tools and methods to track e-mail. The following is just one way to get started and determining if what you receive is authentic or not.

What sits on top of each e-mail is called the header and its contents will vary with the software package. To see these headers you may need to expand the view of your e-mail program to show full headers. Use the Help menu in your e-mail program and search for "headers,"or find "headers" in the index of the "Help" part of the program. Follow the instructions on how to expand your headers.

The following categories may be included in the headers of the e-mail you are examining:

| | |
|---|---|
| Subject | Time |
| Sender name/address | Organization |
| Return path | Comments |
| Recipient name/address | Message ID |
| Date | Signature |

However, all of these components are established by the sender and can therefore be manipulated and falsified. Hence, the sender can say he is mickeymouse@disney.com, and if you do not look into it further, you will not know he is falsifying his information.

Each mail server receiving an e-mail message adds a "Received: from" header to the list of header information. It's possible for end-users to add their own "Received: from" headers to messages. But end-users cannot modify the "Received: from" headers added by the mail servers which deliver the message.

The exact format of "Received: from" headers may vary from site to site, but in general they follow the format below. There may be several "Received: from" lines in one message. The trick is to start from the bottom-most "Received: from" line and work your way up.

The format of "Received: from" headers is as follows:

Received: from reported-sender (DNS-hostname [Connecting-IP-Address]) by mail-server-configured-name (mailer-version/mailer-config-version) with protocol id mail-server-job-identification; time-and-date-stamp.

Here's an example of header information from an e-mail:

```
Received: from .data2know.com [209.166.22.153]
   by data2know.com with ESMTP (SMTPD32-5.05)
   id A8683E70138; Fri, 24 Nov 2000 10:25:28
Message-Id:
<5.0.0.25.2.20001124102827.00a0f9e0@wheresmymailserver.com>
  X-Sender:
X-Mailer: QUALCOMM Windows Eudora Version
   5.0
Date: Fri, 24 Nov 2000 10:28:39 -0500
To: Cyn <cyn@virtuallibrarian.com>
From: HIS <his@data2know.com>
Subject: Testing one two three...
Mime-Version: 1.0
Content-Type: text/plain; charset="us-
   ascii"; format=flowed
X-RCPT-TO: <cyn@virtuallibrarian.com>
X-UIDL: 952340505
Status: U
```

Using the same techniques we used for discovering the registration information of domain names, we can trace the

Internet Protocol (IP) number 209.166.22.153 sent by the user known as *data2know.com*. Go to *http://www.checkdomain.com* and put the number 209.166.22.153 into the box and click search. Take the last entry and match that to *data2know.com*.

Another method is to go to *http://www.samspade.org* and put that number into the WHOIS box and click the "Do Stuff" button. More than likely you will get a match to the person who sent you the e-mail.

Finally, if this is a bit technical for you, you can also try *http://www.spamcop.net*. Go to SpamCop and put your own e-mail address in the box for authorization. It's a free tool but requires your address to avoid spammers abusing the system. You will be e-mailed a web address that you use to go to the actual tool. Once you receive this address, go to the specified site and follow the directions.

## How to Be Efficient on the Internet

*The following advice is from Joe Breskin of Port Townsend, WA (www.breskin.com). Joe uses the Internet to match his customers' technologies with commercial markets.*

One of the most irritating aspects of using computers, especially when searching for someone or something using search engines, is having to enter the same data again and again.

What's wrong with this picture? Aren't computers supposed to help us remember stuff? Why can't it remember what I just typed into that 411 search so I can use it to search the next database? It can and it should. But first you have to create the framework for it to hold this memory.

It doesn't matter much which applications (programs) you have available. All that matters is that you figure out how to do what is described below before you start investing your time in a search that you have to redo because you were not careful enough in writing things down or lost your notes. If you have Windows, you will have "Notepad" because it's part of the operating system (with a Mac it's also called Notepad but you can use SimpleText). It's a very simple text editor but it offers all the performance you need to dramatically improve the effectiveness of your searching.

The simpler the tool that allows the functionality described below, the better it will work. Figure out how to get Notepad open. Create a file. Let's assume you are trying to find a person. Enter all the words you know you will use in your search, each on a separate line.

Start with names and variations: John R. Smith, John Smith, J.R. Smith, J. Smith, Randolph Smith, J. Randolph Smith, Randy Smith, etc.

Then enter all the other things you know: SSN, year of birth, etc.

To use these tools efficiently and effectively, you must learn a couple of fundamental commands and one "Power User" trick. First, save the file. In Notepad, there are mouse moves and keyboard shortcuts. Alt-F, S is the keyboard equivalent of File | Save with the mouse. Put it on a floppy so you can carry it from computer to computer, or e-mail it to yourself so it's in your inbox. Call it NAMES.TXT.

Next, learn to "Copy and Paste." Windows supports three critical combinations of keypresses that you must learn to use the machine effectively. To copy information, highlight it with the mouse or with the keyboard, and press <Ctrl-C> (Control and C).

This copies the highlighted data into a "buffer." To "Paste" a copy of this information from the buffer into a program, put the cursor where you want the data to end up, and press <Ctrl-V> (Control and V). This command copies data from the buffer to the new location.

Any computer which will allow you on the Internet will allow you to have more than one program open at a time. In Windows you "toggle" between two programs (or rotate through several) using <Alt-Tab>. This allows you to have your Notepad running, and your Internet connection running, and to toggle between them. In fact, you will normally have more than one Notepad open. You can use a second to store results you capture off the Internet, and a third to store the URLs of the places you intend to search. To use these tools efficiently, you must <Alt-Tab> (hold down the Alt key and press the Tab key again and again as you watch the screen) to move the focus from one window to the next. This is the basic Power User trick in Windows.

You've already created the NAMES.TXT file. Now create two other Notepad files; call them RESULTS.TXT and URLS.TXT, each in its own copy of Notepad. Practice toggling among them using <Alt-Tab> and copying data from one file to another using <Ctrl-C> and <Ctrl-V>.

This system allows you to get names, correctly and consistently spelled, from your Notepad file to any of the search engines on the Internet. The results off the Internet get pasted right into the RESULTS file. And all those long, meaningless URLs have only to be typed correctly once and used again and again. And new URLs can be typed or copied into the file in the future.

I'm sure you've already been told that the Web is changing rapidly. In particular, most URLs on .com or .edu sites are subject to frequent change without notice. This can create problems if you think of URLs as Dewey decimal numbers in the library or as street addresses in a city. But there are solutions.

A URL is an address, like 1502 Pine Street is an address, but it is also a path. If a URL returns a 404 error ("object not found"), it's possible that most of the address is still good but the actual file has moved.

Imagine a company with a suite of offices. Last weekend they reorganized the files, moving some cabinets into a different room. Your link is to the old location of the files on Floor 2, Room 11, cabinet D-4. Now they are in Room 7 in a different file cabinet. How do you find out if the file you are looking for is really gone or merely moved?

First, you must understand the term "domain name." The domain name is what immediately follows "www." and includes the top-level domain name which is one of the following: .com .net .edu .gov .mil .org. In addition, URLs outside the U.S. have a two-letter country code such as .fi for Finland or .uk for England.

The trick to finding pages that have moved is to edit the URL by removing everything except the domain name and see if that part works. If the domain is still active, add the next layer of the address in an effort to find the file you want. For example, employees may move on to other jobs: so *http://www.seeport.com/staff/breskin/breskin.htm* may disappear, but companies persist, and therefore *http://www.seeport.com* is likely to be there for a long time.

Hope this helps. Good luck in your searching.

*　　*　　*　　*

If you're a newcomer to the Internet, you may soon be hooked. Remember that you still have a job to go to, a family to care for, and those pets to feed. It can become addictive if you're not careful.

Since the Internet is expanding rapidly, there will be tons of newer information available—probably as soon as NOW! But the information provided here should give you plenty to work with for awhile.

Happy hunting!

# Adoption-Related Searches

If you're either adopted and looking for your birth parents or looking for a child you gave up for adoption, take a deep breath, roll up your sleeves and get ready for one of the most difficult kinds of searches. Don't despair, however, because it *is* possible if you approach the search with the right state of mind, the right strategy and the right tools. This chapter will put you on the right track.

There are thousands of adoption-related searchers who either spin their wheels, drive around in circles or just get stuck in the mud. We've picked the brains of some of the nation's best professional and amateur adoption searchers. And the consensus is, although you're probably in for a bumpy ride, you *can* find that person.

"This is probably the most emotional roller coaster ride you'll ever be on," says veteran adoption searcher Mary Lou Kozub. "And it never ends." Over the years, the California-based expert has helped hundreds of people find their birth parents or their birth children. And her work almost always results in success.

The secret to a successful search is a combination of organization, good record keeping, patience, determination, a little luck and a good resource list.

In reality, an adoption-related search is no different than any other search for a person, except for one giant difference—you usually don't know the name of the person you're trying to locate. Of course, that's because some laws, some regulations, some court rulings, and a traditionally secretive attitude has forced the sealing of the most important identifying records you need to find the name of the person you're looking for.

Once you've found that name, this book should make the task of finding him or her a snap of the fingers. Along the way, however, you're likely to run into some pretty powerful emotions—emotions of your adopted family, emotions of your child, emotions of your child's adoptive family or, even worse, your own emotions.

You'll have lots of opportunities to see these emotions as you go through the normal steps to succeeding with an adoption-related search—gathering information, obtaining court papers, trying to get background information from the attorney or agency that handled the adoption, nailing down the name of the person you're tracking, searching for that person, assessing their current situation, planning the actual contact and, possibly along the way, dealing with people who may not be happy about your search.

The most important tool you'll need from the very beginning is a pen and paper. If you don't document every single move you make or piece of information you received, you're likely to go off in a wrong direction or walk right past important clues without seeing them. By keeping a log or journal, and reviewing it after each step, you'll triple your chances of success.

Your actual search must begin with information gathering. If you're searching for your own birth child, you already know the details of the birth and adoption. But if you think you're adopted, how do you really know? Probably your adoptive parents told you. Or maybe you found the adoption papers in that box above their closet. Maybe you suspected it but your folks said, "No way!"

If you're not sure, ask your parents in the most nonthreatening way you can. "Mom, Dad, I'm sure lucky to have you as my parents. I wouldn't trade you for anything in the world. There are some things, though, that make me wonder if maybe you adopted me. If you did, I want to thank you for bringing me into this great family." If that doesn't do it, you may have to look for other clues or talk to other people.

Have a chat with anyone who was in, near or connected to your family at the time you were born—aunts, uncles, grandparents, older siblings, neighbors, family friends, that hairdresser who's been doing Mom's hair for 35 years—anyone. If none of them come clean, the answer may be on your birth certificate, something you don't need anyone's permission to see.

When any baby is born, someone makes out a birth certificate. When that baby is adopted, they make up an amended certificate. Eventually, it gets recorded and the original is sealed. There may be a couple of possible clues on your amended certificate. Now, it won't be labeled "amended birth certificate" because the whole plan was to keep you and others from knowing you were adopted. Look to see whose name is listed as the informant. If the name is typed instead of handwritten, there's a good chance you were adopted. Next, check to see if there's a box that asks the mother how many prior births she's had. If you have older siblings and the certificate says there were no prior births, your older brothers or sisters may have been adopted. There's a good chance you, too, were adopted.

Even better, if the birth certificate of your next youngest sibling shows no prior births, you can be 100% sure you were adopted.

Now that you've determined you were adopted, the information campaign begins. You'll be looking for absolutely any information about your birth and your birth parents. Ultimately, the most important thing to learn is your name at birth or the name of either of your birth parents.

Start by checking around your parents' house. There's a good possibility you'll find a copy of the adoption decree. The information on the decree will save you countless hours of searching.

If you can't find any papers, ask people what they know about the adoption and the people involved. Don't just ask your parents. Ask your relatives, neighbors and family friends.

You've certainly already figured out that your parents might not be doing back flips of joy when you tell them you're searching for your birth parents. And it's a very human reaction. After all, when they adopted you, they certainly harbored fears that the birth mother might want to take you back. The truth is, almost every mother who gives up a baby, at some time wants her baby back, including your own birth mother.

Mary Lou Kozub says adoptive parents need to put the fear in perspective. "Do birth parents want their babies back? Absolutely!" she says. "They're in tremendous pain. It's an amputation from them. They don't know if they've done the right thing. They don't know if the child is okay and healthy. Does the child need anything? Is it in an abusive situation?" The mother did what she thought was best for the child. Does she want her child back? Absolutely.

"But does she *really* want her child back?" Kozub rhetorically asks. "Not in a minute!" Indeed, if she had wanted to take you back, she had ample time to change her mind. The laws are designed to allow a period of time before the adoption is finalized, just in case she changes her mind.

And, years later, the fear that the birth parents might want you back are replaced by fears that you might love your newly-found birth parents more than you love the people who actually raised you. These fears are also quite rational but almost always unfounded. It will be your job to help them erase that fear. If you know or suspect your parents might feel hurt or threatened by your curiosity, you should probably send them a note or letter. A letter can make it a lot easier for you to communicate all the necessary elements because you're not physically present to add to their anxiety. And besides, they won't be able to cut you short or interrupt you. Here's an example you might adapt to your situation:

*Dear Mom and Dad:*

*Words cannot describe how much I love you both. I'm the luckiest kid in the world to have been blessed with such a wonderful family. Sure, like any family, we've had our moments, but I wouldn't trade you for any family in the world.*

*And I'm blessed even more that you actually picked me to be your child. Of all the possible families I could have ended up with, I thank God every day I ended up with you. Thank you for wanting me and loving me so much.*

*It's important to me that you know how happy I am with you—today, yesterday and forever, because I've been feeling compelled over the past few years to learn about my biological parents. Of course it's not because I desire their love or acceptance—after all, they're the ones who didn't want me. But I'm filled with curiosity about my roots, how I may look when I'm older, what medical problems my birth parents may have encountered since my birth—*

*problems that I might be prone to encounter. And I'm curious about any half-brothers or sisters or other relatives I might have. I've done some reading on the subject and I've learned that it's very common for adoptive parents to feel a bit insecure when their adopted children are bit by this common bug. It's a natural fear, but it's almost never a fear that comes true.*

*In your case, you have absolutely nothing to worry about. There is no possible way anyone could eclipse the love I have for you—and always will.*

*With great love, I'm asking you to not only put aside any fears you may have, I'm asking you to actually help me with the search. Hold my hand on my expedition and share the excitement of the search. I can't imagine a greater celebration of the love we share.*

*And even if you can't help me, I pray you'll at least have faith in my love for you and know that you'll always be the only real parents I have.*

*Love,*

*Your kid*

Now that you've successfully recruited your parents, ask them everything you can think of about your birth parents and the circumstances surrounding your adoption. Most important, short of the getting actual names of your birth parents, is finding out who handled the adoption and where.

If you didn't already find the adoption decree among your parents' papers, now is the time to ask them if they might show it to you. If they do, you could possibly skip the next step: seeking the court's adoption files. But you might actually find some interesting things there anyway.

If you didn't find a copy of your amended birth certificate and your parents can't provide one, you can buy it from the vital records office at the town, city or county recorder where you were born. If you don't know your place of birth, the vital records office in the state you were born will sell you a copy of your amended birth certificate. If you don't know the state in which you were born, you might want to ask your parents, relatives or anyone else who would have known your adoptive parents at the time of your birth. Even if no one will tell you, it shouldn't be too tough. If all else fails, use the rest of this book to track down either the marriage certificate of your birth parents or their address at the time you were born.

Your amended birth certificate will also tell you where you were born—at least the county. You need to know this so that you can find the court that approved your adoption.

By now, you certainly know the date and place of your birth—if not the hospital, you should know the county. This is enough information to check in with one of the many birth registries, groups, lists or organizations that try to match both parties of an adoption, if both parties submit their names and any information they might have. There's a good chance either your birth mother or father or your birth child has submitted or will submit their names to the list. If there's a match, the registry will let you know.

By far the best registry is the International Soundex Reunion Registry. Since they seem to register the most names, they have a better success rate than others. However, it never hurts to put your name in as many registries as possible. Check the adoption references at the end of this chapter. Or contact a search professional in your area and ask them to point you toward nearby registries.

Also, you should search the Internet using a good search engine (see Chapter 5). Use the name of your state and the words "adoption, registry, search, birth and parents." You'll quickly come up a wonderful list of people and organizations willing to help. Once you've registered, you might get lucky and be reunited with that birth parent or birth child even before you've completed the search. But don't just sit and wait, get back to work on your search.

Next you should call the county clerk in that county. The clerk is usually the clerk of the county-wide court. Ask the clerk which court finalized adoptions at the time of your birth. If the county clerk doesn't know, call any county court and ask the clerk there.

The next step is to petition the court that handled your adoption. If you can, go there in person, but either way you should make the request (in writing) for the entire adoption case file, including the petition for adoption and the final decree of adoption. It's most likely they're not going to give you the whole file, but you never know. Why limit yourself? They might just throw in the relinquishment papers. If you haven't already seen them, you will have scored a home run.

It's usually better to go in person and hand them your letter petitioning your file. If they say it will take awhile, you should tell them in a very pleasant and patient manner, "Oh, no problem. I can wait."

Always ask for several copies. They have no right to ask you why you need them. Mary Lou Kozub advises her clients to simply tell the clerk it's for "judicial need." They may ask you to show some identification—that's no problem—and they may ask you if you want it certified. There's really no need for certification, which costs more anyway.

If you're lucky, they'll prepare the papers right in front of you. Be sure to wear your best glasses. There is certain information they are not supposed to give you, so they'll have to remove it. They may do this in a variety of ways. But your best bet is to watch like a hawk, just in case you can read something before they try to obliterate it.

If you're lucky, they'll use something such as a black crayon. That means later you can use a sharp razor blade to gently scrape away the crayon marks. Practice it carefully before you put the blade to the important part of the form.

They may also use a permanent marker. That's fine too. You'll find that you can hold the paper up to the right light and read much or all of what they're trying to hide. Unfortunately, with so many people doing what you're doing, they've wised up and found a way to prevent you from reading what they've covered up—they blacken out the key words with a permanent marker and then photocopy that doctored copy. Once in a great while, however, you can still see a very faint image of the original letters—even though it's a copy of a doctored copy. Sometimes just figuring out one letter can be helpful.

But assuming the worst, if you ended up with a copy that was effectively censored, you may still be able to figure out some things. If they used a standard typewriter without proportional spacing, you can sometimes count the number of letters a blacked out word must have had. Maybe they didn't completely cover the bottom tail of the letters g, j, p, q or y. Or maybe you'll see the exposed tops of the letters b, d, f, h, k, l or t. Sometimes they'll overlook an entire word, sentence or other clue—sometimes they'll inadvertently give you key names and addresses.

The Final Adoption Decree should name the agency that handled your adoption, depending on the type of adoption involved. Generally, there are three types of adoptions—private adoptions, independent adoptions and county adoptions.

In a private adoption, a private or religious agency acts as an intermediary. The people there take the baby from the hospital and provide foster care for as long as it takes to match the baby with what they think is the right family. The baby could be in a foster home for only a very short time or for many months.

The independent adoption involves no agency—government or private. Often it's arranged by an attorney and the doctor. When the baby is born, the hospital hands over the baby to either the attorney or to the adoptive parents. But it can also be done without any outside assistance. It's possible for the birth mother or birth parents to come to an agreement with the adoptive parents-to-be. They all go down to the county court and petition the judge directly.

In a county adoption, one agency (usually a government body) handles the adoptions for the entire county. Sometimes an agency will take care of the adoptions for two or more counties. Check with the court in the county you were born to determine what agency handles adoptions

The Final Adoption Decree will usually name the agency if it was an agency adoption, the attorney if it was a private adoption, and the county itself if it was a county adoption. If no such information shows up on the decree, it was probably an independent adoption.

No matter which type of adoption occurred, the state in which you were born almost always keeps a master file of all adoptions. You can write to the appropriate state agency and find out how the adoption was handled. If it was a county adoption or private adoption, you may be able to skip this step. But if it was an independent adoption, this is where you must go to get your background information. It's a good idea, however, to check in with the state even if it was a county or private adoption—just in case the birth child or the birth parents have been there before you and completed a waiver of rights. That means they're hoping you may be looking for them and have told the state it's okay to put you in touch with each other. If they haven't, your waiver of rights will work the same way for you if the birth child or birth parents check with the state before you've found them. And no matter what type of adoption was involved, you should request that the state send you your background information. It will provide you with valuable clues about the birth child or the birth parents. And if the adoption involved was a county or private adoption, you'll also need to check with the government or private agency that processed your adoption. If you didn't already learn it, the state's file should reflect which agency handled the adoption.

When you approach the agency that handled the adoption, they'll probably ask you to complete a waiver of confidentiality or some other consent form and sign it in front of a notary public. The form may ask you what other names you've been known by in the past. Even though you may already know your name at birth, do not provide that name. Based on experience, many agencies will be more vague if they're aware you know your name at birth. That's because they've usually dealt with scores of people looking for their birth parents and they tend to become unnecessarily protective. Some even treat the records as if they're actually sealed.

"There are only two things that are sealed—the court file and the original birth certificate," says Mary Lou Kozub, "but the agencies often interpret this to mean your entire record is sealed. In some counties, it will take a year and a half to get your background information—that is, if you bug them three or four times. If you don't bug them at all, it'll take two years. I recommend you bug them once a week."

When you receive the background information you may get what's called non-identifying information—information that won't clue you regarding the actual names of the parties involved. So be sure to request all the information, not just the non-identifying information. Again, it never hurts to ask.

You will get certain information about the birth mother and birth father—possibly including their nationality, ethnicity, religion, occupation, number of brothers or sisters, ages of their parents, education level, medical conditions, physical descriptions and sometimes their actual ages or dates of birth.

But don't be satisfied with just the minimum information—go for more. Ask lots of questions. "Could you give me my mother's first name? How about her initials? Is her name in the first half of the alphabet? The second? Grandparents names? First names? Occupations?" There's a very good chance they'll give you much or all of this information if you are politely persistent.

With any luck, by now you've learned enough to piece together an identity of either your birth parents, your child's adoptive parents or someone else who would know. You may have to stay up a few nights going over the information again and again until you discover a clue you didn't see before. This is a good time to call on trusted friends to help you brainstorm.

And maybe it's time to approach your adoptive parents once again. When you show them how much energy you've put into this, and you share what information you did get, they may realize you're serious and reconsider their stand.

If you're totally stuck and you haven't been able to learn the name of either your birth parents, birth child or adoptive parents, you may need to call for reinforcements. Take the information you have to your nearest genealogical library. They may have important birth, marriage or death indices that can help you take the next step. Also, visit your nearest large library or university library and ask the reference librarian for some help.

There are various support groups who may help you further the search. The Alma Society is in most major cities. For a reasonable fee, they'll help you with additional training, advice and moral support. See Appendix A and the end of this chapter.

If all else fails, you may have to hire a professional adoption searcher (see Appendix A). It's certainly not cheap, but if you've done most of the legwork yourself, you should be able to substantially reduce the costs.

If you've learned the first or last name and the date of birth of the person you're seeking, you may want to contact a professional searcher. See Chapter 4 and Appendix E for more information.

By now you should have been able to identify and locate the birth parents or birth child—either through your own efforts or with help from a professional searcher. Now comes the real roller coaster ride. This is where you ask yourself questions such as, "Will they want to see me? Does their current family know I exist? Will they reject me? Will they want a relationship? Will I get too attached to them? What if it's the wrong person I found? Should I spy on them first? Should I knock on the door or call them? Write them a letter, maybe? Should I let someone else contact them for me? Do I go there alone? What do I say? How should I act? Why did I even start this search in the first place? Do I even have the right to see them? Can I force myself on them? What if they deny they're the ones I'm looking for?"

From here on, there's no set formula. It all depends on your situation and what you've learned about their situation. It's a good time to read Chapter 7 on how to check someone out. It's important to do your best to get a feel for what their world is today. Are they married? Do they have children? Half-siblings? Are they healthy? Your own research should give you some clues. Have they been divorced? Can you identify someone—such as an ex-spouse or the new husband or wife of an ex-spouse—who might discreetly paint you a picture of the current situation and the knowledge other family members might have about either the baby they gave up or the very fact that someone was adopted in the first place. You run the risk, of course, of that person getting to the person before you can. But if you're genuinely honest and appear compassionate, you can probably get that person to keep quiet.

Investigative reporter Don Ray has helped scores of people locate and make contact with birth parents or children separated by adoptions. He believes that if he uses his experience and sensitivity to make the first contact with the birth parent or child he can make it easier for both parties—the searcher and the person sought.

"By being an intermediary, I can make certain there's only one person who's emotionally charged during that crucial first contact," he says. "I can be vague enough when I call to make sure I'm calling at the right time and talking to the right person. And when I explain that their child or parent is looking for them, I can also—as an outsider—do a better job of telling them the wonderful things about their child or parent and put their mind at ease about the normal fears they might have. I can assure them the person is not going to barge in on their family and disrupt things. I can help them plan a first meeting that's in a private place or at a more convenient time.

"Then, of course, I can go back to the searcher and assure him or her that the person they've found is, indeed, the right person and that the parent or child is anxious to meet them again. In all my searches, there's only been one person, a birth mother, who initially didn't want contact. She had a family of her own now and hadn't told them about the little baby girl she had given up for adoption. But after she thought about it for a day, she changed her mind and called her birth daughter."

As a professional searcher, Mary Lou Kozub will not make the actual contact. Instead, she coaches the searcher and leaves it to him or her to decide when and how to contact their birth child or birth parent.

"There's no right way of making contact," she says. "Every case is different. Sometimes it's better to do it by phone, other times it's best to do it in person." She says that writing to the birth parent or child is at the bottom of her list.

Most seem to agree that, in general, a face-to-face meeting is probably the best. It's quite easy to hang up the phone on someone and make them go away. But it's really hard to close the door on someone who you know is of your own flesh and blood. You should carefully plan the first contact. Through your background work, try to determine when he or she is home alone. That's always better.

When you make the initial contact, you may be very nervous. If someone else answers the door, you'll have to ask if the person you're seeking is there. If not, you can politely ask when he or she will be home and say you'll come back. They're probably going to ask what it's all about. You can tell them an old friend is trying to make contact and that you'd rather talk to him or her personally. Or, you could leave your name and phone number and ask that they call you back. The chances are your name will mean nothing to the person who answered the door. But it's quite likely a birth parent will know or suspect what it's all about. This technique allows him or her to call you back when it's safe or convenient. If it's a birth child you're looking for, remember that they may not know they're even adopted. This is why it's a good idea to learn from someone else just how much the birth child knows.

If the person you're seeking answers the door, you must make sure you can isolate them long enough to safely explain what you're up to. Ask them if they're alone. If not, ask if they'll come outside or if there's a place where you could talk privately. Let them know that what you have to say is very personal. They'll surely comply.

We suggest you then ask them if they are the "Susan Smith" born on a certain date. When they say they are, you should tell them your name and that you've been looking for them for a long time. By now, it's almost certain they're going to know what's coming next. "You gave a child up for adoption in 19__. I'm that child and I wanted to let you know I turned out okay. I've been well-taken care of and I realized that I wanted to, at least once, get a chance to see you and thank you for bringing me into the world." By saying this right away, you'll be alleviating many of the first fears they will have. They've wondered a million times if they made the right decision to give you up, if you've had a good life, if you're healthy, if you're even alive, if you're going to make trouble for them, if you want a relationship and more. This approach will answer most of the questions they've had.

If other people are present, the person you are contacting may want to get back in touch with you at a later time. Be sure to have a card ready that has your name, address and telephone number written on it. It should be small enough for them to put in their pocket in case they don't want to tell their family about you. You could also jot down a short note with kind, warm, nonthreatening information on it—about yourself, things you've done, where you've lived and even a few more words that will assure them you're not going to force yourself on them. It might not hurt to also mention on the note that, if they call you, it will easier than you coming back at another time. If they're reluctant to see you or have you in their life, this will make them want to deal with you on the phone—even if it's only to keep you away. And they will probably be calling when it's okay for them to talk. You'll then have another chance to put their mind at ease and assure them you're not going to make trouble.

Remember that if you're looking for a birth father, he might not know he's a birth father. It's usually better to first find the birth mother or people close to her so that you can find out if Daddy knows he's a daddy. But don't worry too much. If you make the contact discreetly enough, you can drop the bomb on him fairly gently. Don't feel too much guilt for letting him know. After all, he *is* your father and he should *know* he's your father.

If you're seeking a birth child, it's much more important that you find out if they know they're adopted. If they're still living with their adoptive parents, think very carefully about the ramifications of making contact. If they don't know they're adopted, you could do some immediate harm. A mother knows when she's given up her child for adoption and often thinks about the child. However, some adoptees make it to adulthood not knowing they were adopted.

If your birth child is under age, we suggest you wait until she is at least 18 before you attempt to make contact. And, again, if she is still living with the adoptive parents, consider waiting until she moves out. When you do make contact, remember that he or she may deny or refuse to believe she was adopted. You could be walking into a land mine here. We would even suggest you go to an adoption search consultant, explain what you know of the situation, and ask for advice. It would be worth a consultation fee to know you weren't about to inflict undue pain or anxiety on your own child.

If you make contact on the telephone, be sure to identify the person by name and date of birth or some other way, and then tell them your name and ask them to write down your phone number in case you get disconnected. This is very, very important. In the event they don't want to talk or can't talk, they'll have a way to reach you later if they want. Nothing is more frustrating than to hear from someone and not be able to get back in touch with them.

If you are searching for your birth parent, let them know you're trying to contact the parent who brought you into the world. You want to thank them for giving you life and let them know you're okay. Tell them you've always dreamed of seeing them in person, at least once, so you could assure them you've had a good life and you turned out to be a good person. Also, you might tell them you're very curious about your birth parents and want to know some vital things about their health—things that one day might affect you. Tell them you want to know about your own genealogy and about possible half-brothers and sisters. And you can tell them that they're not obligated to have any kind of a relationship with you, but the door's open at your end.

If you write to your birth parent or birth child, be aware of how every word may affect them. As strange as it might seem, avoid telling them you love them—after all, how do you know you love them? Love usually requires some kind of relationship, and you don't even know them. And while your feelings and desires are important, keep in mind that *they* play a part in this too, and they may not share your feelings. Remember that you have every right to know who your birth parents are and to have certain information about them. And your birth child has every right to know his or her birth parents, but may not want to exercise that right, at least not right now. Be prepared for the possibility they may not want any part of meeting you. But don't close the doors—there could be a change of heart. People hopefully become wiser as they grow older.

The more compassion and consideration you show, the greater your chances are of having a positive, heartwarming reunion—and perhaps, many more.

## National Adoption Organizations

This is a national organization that brings together local levels of adoption researchers, support groups and individuals committed to adoption issues:

The American Adoption Congress
1025 Connecticut Ave, N.W., #1012
Washington, DC 20036
(202) 483-3399
*www.AmericanAdoptionCongress.org*

## National Adoption Registries

ISSR is a free national registry for birth children and birth parents. Formed in 1975.

International Soundex Reunion Registry (ISRR)
PO Box 2312
Carson City, NV 89702-2312
(702) 882-7755
*www.plumsite.com/issr*

ALMA is a nonprofit membership organization with a registry, a newsletter, and a searching guide. It also sponsors local chapters and search workshops. Formed in 1971.

Adoptees Liberty Movement Assn (ALMA)
PO Box 85
Denville, NJ 07834
*www.almanet.com*

# Background Checking Using Public Records

Most of this book finds answers to the question,"Where is he?" Sometimes, however, you may be more concerned with the question, "Who is he?" or even, "What is he?" Finding these things out about a person is done through *background checking* and involves extensive use of public records.

Who might you be wanting to check out? Could be a prospective tenant for one of your rental properties. Maybe it's someone you're considering hiring. How about that slick young man who wants to date your daughter? Or that even slicker, older man who's making eyes at your widowed mother (or is he making eyes at her savings account)? Maybe it's someone from whom you may want to buy something or to whom you might want to sell something. Then there's that ex-husband you suspect is spending like a sailor while he tells the judge he can barely afford the alimony or child support. It could be a noisy neighbor who doesn't want to turn the stereo down at two in the morning. And, of course, it could very well be that baby-sitter, baseball coach, den mother or even the good ol' Reverend/Rabbi/Father Dave.

Depending upon how motivated you are, you could just make a phone call or two, or you could spend months building an impressive dossier on someone.

Where to start? Start with what you know—a name, a date of birth, an address, a Social Security number, a license plate number, whatever. Any of these items will probably lead you to a good identity of someone. Once you've identified the person you can turn to one or more of the resources or strategies below.

The *telephone book*. Always look there first. As private as people are getting to be, the phone book is still pretty fat. He may only list his name and phone number, but it's a start. If you can learn the address, all the better. If you're doing a full background investigation, be sure to look for older phone books or city directories. Your phone company may have them. Sometimes they're at the local or regional library, the historical society, a nearby genealogy library or even at the local chamber of commerce. Your state library may also have a collection of old directories. Don't forget to ask about *criss-cross directories* (or reverse directories). These books are sorted not by name, but by address and/or phone numbers. It never hurts to find out who someone's neighbors were 20 years ago and what they might have to say about your subject today.

Armed with a name (and better, with an address or date of birth) you can probably view the listings at the *registrar of voters*. You'll probably find these files at the city or township level if you're in the eastern part of the U.S. and at the county level as you move further west. The office in charge of voter records should provide you with the person's name, address, prior address, date of birth, place of birth, political leanings, occupation, a copy of his signature, phone number (sometimes it's optional; often it's an unlisted number), the date he first registered, sometimes a Social Security number or sometimes even a physical description. While you're there, you can probably find out who else is voting at that address.

*Property tax records* could be at the town, city or county level of government. Usually, you can access the specific file on someone by knowing either the person's name, the property address, its legal description or its file number (often the number consists of a book, page and parcel number). Also, if you can find the property on any map, it will lead you to the file. When you access the file, you should be able to find out the assessed value of the land as well as the improvements (buildings) and any exemptions. You may also find reference to the deed of which the assessor received a copy—the deed upon which they assessed the value of the property. Look for an instrument or document number. That's probably the number the recorder of deeds assigned to the document. It will come in handy when you visit the recorder's office.

Also, keep in mind that you can go back in time at the assessor's office and see how long the person has been paying taxes on the property. It's a good place to look for current and former neighbors. They might be fun to track down for a little chat.

While you're at the assessor's office you may find reference to the person's tax payment history. If it's not there, it's probably at the office of the tax collector—just down the hall.

Next you should visit the *recorder of deeds*. Here you can look for that *deed* referenced over at the assessor's office. The deed will show you from whom they bought the property, when, and for how much. The actual price may not show up on the deed, but there's a good chance there's reference to some transfer tax that you can use to compute the purchase price. Be sure to look for accompanying *deeds of trust* (mortgages). Usually folks have to borrow money from some lending institution when they buy a house. You'll find that agreement filed not too far from the deed. Look closely, because he may have had to borrow from a couple of people to come up with the purchase price. Look for second, third and even fourth deeds of trust. They'll clearly tell you how much money he borrowed.

While you're there, look for *notices of default* (when they got a bit behind on the payments), *notices of sale* (when they got really behind), *mechanics liens* (when they had work done on their house and still owed money to the contractor), *state and federal tax liens*, *abstracts of judgments* (when a judge settles property ownership disputes), *bonds* and *reconveyances* (notices that they've paid off trust deeds). You may also find that he has recorded his *military discharge papers* (DD 214) so that he can easily make legal copies in the future. That will really help you if you want to dig into his military records.

While you're at the recorder's office (again, more likely to be at the city or township level as you get closer to the Atlantic seaboard and at the county level the more you travel west) you should look for *vital records*—birth certificates, marriage certificates and death certificates, if they're accessible in your state.

The person's *birth certificate* will tell you about his parents, his doctor, indications of older siblings, his first home address and much more. The birth certificates of his children are likely to give you a good work address for him and the children's mother(s), as well as an indication of other, older children.

His *marriage certificate* will also indicate where he and his wife were working and living at the time they were married, names of both of their parents, possibly some religious reference and the all-important names and addresses of the best man and maid of honor. If he's been divorced, there's a good chance you can find his ex-wife for some good tidbits. Ex-spouses can make great victims and enemies. Victims and enemies are wonderful to talk to when you're backgrounding someone, because they are usually more likely to want to give you some juicy information, and they're less likely to go squealing that you were asking about him.

Keep in mind, however, that ex-spouses sometimes have kids, child support or alimony that bonds them. An even better person to track down is the person who stood up for the ex-wife. She's most likely the woman's best friend. And while the ex-wife might not want to shove any dirt your way, her best friend is usually more than happy to slip you word on the slimier side of the guy who screwed over her best friend.

Obviously you won't be looking at the *death certificate* of any living person you're checking out, but sometimes it's worth while to look at the death certificates of his parents or grandparents. It could lead you to the names of other family members, coroners' case files, and clues as to where to look for probate files (we'll cover them when we get to the courts).

Your city or county might also require folks doing business to file *fictitious name statements*—sometimes called assumed name statements. These will give you indications of the kinds of businesses he might have started up, the structure of the true owner (individual, corporation, partnership, etc.) and the names and address of all the parties involved. Again, find people he was in business with in the past—but not today—and you're likely to find a victim or enemy just bubbling over with information.

Your subject might have had to get a business permit or *business license* to run the business. Look at the township, city or county level for these.

Before you leave the recorder's office, ask them where people register their *animal licenses*. Usually records of pet licenses are a matter of public record.

Also, you might want to look for *building permits* that were taken out when they built that addition or added that pool.

Now it's time to visit the *courts*. Courts at any level can be gold mines of information. Start with *small claims court*. Trust us—anyone who's ever filed a small claims suit is a motivated, and probably frustrated, person. They probably won their case against your subject but collected little or nothing. The anger and hatred it leaves can outlive nuclear waste. Track down the other party in a small claims case and you'll have fountains of information overflowing in your direction.

Check the files at the nearest *traffic court* and you'll find the actual copies of traffic citations and possibly arrests for driving under the influence of something. This can be a wonderful indicator of someone's reliability. You should question the character of anyone with more than one DUI or more than a few traffic violations over a short period of time.

Now you should check the township, city and county levels of courts for civil filings, criminal filings, family law filings and probate cases. You may find these at more than one level of court, i.e., justice court, municipal court, district court, superior court, etc.

If your subject is involved in *civil cases*, he has either been accused of doing something that damaged someone or he, himself, might be quick to sue. Read the files thoroughly and jot down the names of all opposing parties and attorneys.

*Criminal cases* should be important to you. If you find his name in the index, be sure to pull the file. Is it really the same person? What was he charged with? Was he convicted? What was the sentence? Any probation or parole indicated? It's another great place to find victims and enemies.

*Family law cases* (divorce, dissolution, custody disputes) are usually jewels. Divorce cases, especially, have more accusations per square inch than probably any other file. Why is that? When they fall in love they can see no wrong in their sweetheart. Then, after a few years of marriage, they (to put it mildly) have changed their mind. The good news for you is that they often write down all those nasty thoughts and they end up in the case file. Yep, before you decide to marry someone, find out how they acted or how they were perceived at the time of their last breakup. Caution—this can be sobering, but better to know now than later. On the other hand, you'll probably not believe anyone could say such rotten things about your current flame. And, to be completely honest, in many cases such accusations are not true. But don't say we didn't warn you!

When someone dies, the courts often get involved to help decide how to distribute the person's money and property. This is called a *probate file*. This is where you might want to check out what happened to your subject's father or grandfather. Remember the old adage: "Where there's a will, there's a relative." You'll usually find that the person's will is part of the file. It will not only tell you who all the heirs are, but who was the most and least popular in the eyes of the dearly departed. Let's say your subject was left $50,000 by his father and an equal amount went to each of his three sisters. But he specifically wrote brother Bob out of the will. Mark our words, brother Bob will sing. You'll probably even learn how many times your subject wet the bed when he was a kid. Victims and enemies. They're the greatest.

The probate file can also be a good way of finding someone's assets. Maybe they didn't tell anyone they inherited a carload of money.

A lot of people overlook the many ways the average Joe can interact with the U.S. District Court. What ways? He could have been a party to a civil suit, he could have been arrested by federal authorities, he could have filed for bankruptcy, he may have taken the IRS to task (or vice versa) by going straight to U.S. Tax Court, or he could have gone to Naturalization Court in hopes of becoming a U.S. citizen.

*Bankruptcy files* have the best information—lots of information about finances, assets, and of course, victims and enemies. Don't forget to look for more than one. Some people make a career out of going broke.

There is at least one U.S. District and one U.S. Bankruptcy Court in each state. Some of the larger states have several courts. Unfortunately, you will have to go to the federal court your subject was involved with, or hire a researcher to go there for you.

*The Sourcebook of Federal Courts, U.S. District and Bankruptcy* by BRB Publications, and the *United States Court Directory*, available from the Government Printing Office (see Chapter 9), both list U.S. courts. You may also contact the Federal Information Center for a specific court's address (see Chapter 9).

Next you should consider searching for *licenses*. Think about the kinds of licenses you have and others he may have.

He probably has a *drivers license*, but what's public varies from state to state. If you have access to drivers license records, you're likely to find current and previous addresses, former names, physical descriptions, date of birth, other states in which he was once licensed, restrictions (glasses, limited driving hours or areas), records of traffic citations, accidents, and drunk driving arrests. Remember, if you learn about citations from his driving record, ask for the court that convicted him and the citation (or docket) number.

Usually the same motor vehicle department will have the *vehicle records*. Be sure to ask about other cars, motorcycles, trailers, boats, mobile homes, motor homes or anything else your state licenses.

What other licenses might your subject have? Is he a realtor, doctor, private investigator, automobile repairman, barber, chiropractor or funeral director? These and many more occupations require licenses—usually at the state level.

Does he fly or own a plane? Check with the Federal Aviation Administration. Is he a ham radio operator? Check with the Federal Communication Commission. Does he sell insurance? Check with your state's insurance commission. Does he practice law? Check with the state bar association.

It doesn't hurt to check with your *secretary of state*. This office keeps track of corporations, limited partnerships and limited liability companies. It should also keep track of Uniform Commercial Code filings. These are public notices people are required to file when they use anything other than real estate or vehicles for collateral for a loan.

If you think your subject once ran for office or supported a politician or ballot measure, be sure to check for *political contributions* at the city, county, state and federal levels.

If he's possibly involved in any big way with a publicly-held corporation, you may just find reference to him, his assets or salary in the files of the Securities and Exchanges Commission.

If you think he was ever in the military, you should check that out too. See Chapter 8 for details on how to request *military records*. Keep in mind that many men are claiming they were combat veterans when, in reality, they never set foot in a combat area. Some were never even in the military.

Another area in which people are likely to fudge information is the field of *education*. You can call almost any college or university, ask for the admissions office, and they'll confirm that someone attended that institution. You may be able to learn the dates they attended, their major field of study, when they graduated and with what degree. Once you find out what his major was, be sure to call back to the university and ask for that department. Many times the history department or the psychology department or the political science department will keep records about the students in their area of study. We've had luck finding out about prior addresses, off-campus employment and other activities this way.

You should also check your subject's *employment record.* Find a previous employer and ask for a copy of his resumé or application. You'll be surprised—sometimes they'll give it up.

You should also look for things written about the person you're backgrounding. Check with the local papers where he's lived or worked. Check any *publications* that deal with his specialty. If he's an umpire, see if he's been written up in any umpire publications. There isn't any area of interest that doesn't have one or more specialty publications. Check with your reference librarian for help. There are "Who's Who" books for just about every industry, profession or activity. While you're at the library, by the way, check to see if he's had to pay any fines on overdue library books. The information on his actual library card is not likely a matter of public record, but the payment of fines probably is.

No background check on a person is complete without checking him out on the *Internet.* Run his name through at least four search engines to see if he shows up on any World Wide Web sites. They use a web-crawler program to see if he has used his computer to chat with people in any of the thousands of news groups—these are groups of people who often send e-mail messages to large numbers of people in their specialty or interest group. You'll be amazed at the information people will divulge about themselves over the Internet without realizing or caring that anyone else can search for anything they've written.

If you're really serious about learning everything about this person, you might want to consider talking to people who were or are in contact with him. Of course, you run the risk of him finding out you're digging into his life, but that may not be a problem. Sometimes, in fact, his knowledge that you're doing such a thorough background search will bring a quick end to whatever problem you're trying to solve.

There are many legal, ethical, acceptable and appropriate reasons to gather information about someone. You must take care to respect the person's privacy. Remember, the main reason to check out someone *should be* to protect yourself.

Chapter 8

# *Military Connections*

Are you considering skipping this chapter? Before you do, you might want to read this short story:

It wasn't too long ago that 68-year-old Millie Dawson called us to ask for help. She was in very poor health and afraid she might not live long enough to locate her half-sister—a woman she'd been trying to find for fifty years.

Millie had grown up in an average American family. Her parents were happily married. She was their only child. After high school graduation in 1943, she enlisted in the Women's Army Corps. Just before Millie left for basic training, her mother revealed a startling story about giving birth to a baby girl before she was married to Millie's father.

She had become involved with a man and become pregnant. Millie's mother immediately put the baby up for adoption, but kept track of the little girl—even secretly visited her over the years. Millie was shocked. Neither she nor her father had ever known of Millie's half-sister.

Millie's mother decided to tell Millie about the baby after she had a premonition that she would never see Millie again. Millie should know the truth, she thought.

Millie was stationed in Europe following basic training. That's when she received the sad news—her mother had died back home. The premonition had come true.

Millie was forever haunted by her mother's story. She had been so caught off guard at the time, that she couldn't remember all the details her mother had told her. But she always dreamed of finding her sister—even though she couldn't remember her name. The only thing she recalled was that in 1940 her sister married a sailor named Barry Smith who lived in Savannah, Georgia. Throughout the years, Millie tried in vain to find him, hoping he was still married to her sister—or, at least, knew where she was.

It was a desperate, tearful Millie who finally came to us for help. She, herself, was now dying. She cried as she told her story. She feared it would be impossible to find her sister in time.

Right away we contacted the Department of Veterans Affairs, but there were just too many Barry Smiths. Next, we searched a national telephone directory and found no Barry Smiths in Savannah but, of course, hundreds all over the United States—far too many to contact. We figured Barry Smith was probably born between 1916 and 1920, so we plugged his name and age range into several proprietary computer databases. The results? There were only six Barry Smiths in the country who were the right age. We wrote to the VA Records Processing Center in St. Louis to learn that, of the six Barry Smiths, only one was in the Navy during WWII.

When we contacted him, he told us how in 1940 he had

married an adopted woman—Mary Wilson. They were now divorced, but he was still in touch with her.

"I can't believe it," Mary screamed. "I've been searching for her for years!" She told us a story that matched Millie's to the letter. Mary had been adopted shortly after she was born, but she had, indeed, seen her birthmother several times before she got married, but then they lost contact. She knew she had a half sister, but had never seen her.

The happy sisters talked for the first time on the phone. But it only took a few weeks for Mary to show up at Millie's door. The two were able to get to know and love each other over the next few months. Despite her courage, Millie lost her battle against death. But before she slipped away, she told Mary and the others close to her that she could now die in peace—after 50 years, she finally found her sister.*

Since we are recognized as experts at tracking down people with a military connection, this chapter will be even more detailed than the others. All of the information here and much more is in our book *How to Locate Anyone Who Is or Has Been in the Military* by Lt. Col. Richard S. Johnson. This chapter will help you locate people on active duty, retired folk, reservists and veterans or help you acquire a mound of military records.

Did your subject have any connection with the armed services? Or, as in the story of Millie and Mary, is there someone in his life who is or was once connected with the military? Maybe you're cursed with one of those tough cases where no other methods have worked. The military angle could be your winning connection.

If you've ever been a member of the armed services, you'll probably agree with this age-old G.I. expression: "In the mil-

*The story of Millie and Mary was adapted from a story Richard S. Johnson first wrote for his "Searching" column in *Reunions Magazine*.

itary, there are three ways of doing things—the right way, the wrong way and the military way." Some of the truest words ever spoken—especially when it comes to tracking down current or former military people.

If you've never been in the military, you'd logically think that if someone was stationed at, say, Ft. Dix, New Jersey, then the first place you'd check would be at Ft. Dix, right? Surely, Ft. Dix would keep track of all the people ever stationed there, right? It's only logical, right?

Wrong! Why? Because it is logical—much too logical. Most people aren't aware that it was General George Washington who outlawed all things logical in the U.S. military. Or did he do it by executive order when he was President? Regardless, it's been SOP (Standard Operating Procedure) since before 2LTs (Second Lieutenants) began ordering PFCs (Privates First Class) to a week of KP (Kitchen Police) for going AWOL (Absent Without Leave) to avoid having to eat another portion of SOS (Nope, sorry! Any former G.I. can explain it to you.).

The military gives the responsibility of record-keeping to the actual unit or ship. And the military way makes sense in this case. Military units, by their very design, are transient—always ready to move. The bases and forts and ships are more like motels, only much larger.

But very logical people come to us all the time asking if, say, Ft. Dix is still operating. They're looking for someone who was stationed there in 1964. Some folks have already packed up the car to drive to the installation on their vacation, all with the assumption they'll find reference to their friend or relative in some file there.

But there are no such records at military installations. In 1964 there may have been twenty different units stationed at Ft. Dix. When the units eventually left, they took their records with them. What most people need to find is a unit roster (a list of a unit's personnel that includes each person's complete legal name and their service number. See page 134). Many unit rosters and morning reports (daily records of personnel joining or leaving the unit) are housed at the National Personnel Records Center in St. Louis, Missouri. You can view them in person, hire someone near St. Louis to pull the files for you, or just write and request a copy.

But the energy you put into getting your hands on the unit rosters and morning reports is energy well spent. They turned out to hold the key to success for a Vietnam-born Amerasian woman, Sue, who called us. She was looking for her birth father—an American military man who served in Vietnam. The only information she had about him was that his name was Mike and he was from Florida. If it wasn't for the military connection, Sue would have been out of luck.

Fortunately, she had an important clue—she knew where he was stationed when he had met her mother. She first had to find out what units were stationed in that area at that time. Then she wrote for unit rosters for each of the units, specifying the month and year. Once she received the rosters, she highlighted only the listings of the names Mike and Michael. Then she had to determine which of the Mikes on that list was from Florida. Actually, it was easy. Service numbers issued in Florida contained a unique sequence of numbers. Only one of the men had entered the military in Florida.

She quickly called the Department of Veterans Affairs who confirmed that they had his current address. She then wrote the letter (forwarded by the VA) that would introduce herself to the man who, as it turned out, had not known he had fathered a child. In this case, it was the military connection that brought Sue and her father together.

If you already have enough identifying information, you can go directly to the appropriate military branch. Each branch has a world-wide locator for locating active duty, reserve and retired military. The folks at the world-wide locators will either forward a letter or tell you the unit to which he's currently assigned—even though in some cases they'll only tell you about units assigned in the United States. If you would rather bypass the active duty locator, then refer to Chapter 5 (Using the Internet) and search the active duty military list yourself.

If you want them to forward a letter on your behalf, simply place it in a sealed, stamped envelope. Put your name and return address in the upper left-hand corner. In the center of the envelope put the person's rank and full name followed by the Social Security number or date of birth (if you know it). On a separate sheet of paper put everything you know that might help the locator identify the person, such as: name, rank, Social Security number, branch of service, date of birth (or a good guess), sex, whether he was an officer or enlisted (if you don't know the rank), your best guess as to the date he entered the service, his last known assignment and anything else you might know about him.

Then put that sealed envelope into a larger one—preferably business size (No. 10), along with the fact sheet and a check for the search fee ($3.50) made payable to Treasurer of the U.S. They'll waive the fee if you're currently active, reserve, National Guard, retired military or a family member but be sure to let them know this on the fact sheet (show your rank and Social Security number or relationship). On the outer envelope include your name and return address. Address it to the appropriate armed forces locator.

If the people at the military locator can identify the individual, they'll forward it. If the person gets your letter and never replies, you may be out of luck. The military can't force anyone to write. If they can't identify the person, they'll return your letter with an explanation. Common problems include: the locator can't identify him without a Social Security number (especially if you're looking for a common name), he has already been discharged, you gave them the wrong Social Security number or he's no longer alive.

Just to keep you from being in suspense, you might want to staple a stamped postcard—addressed to you—to the letter. Consider having fun with it to encourage him to send it back right away. On the back side write something such as:

<Please check one and drop this card in the mail.>

Dear [Your name]:

[ ] Wow! Great to hear from you. I m busy but I ll write soon.

[ ] Wow! Great to hear from you. Here s my phone number -- call me ____________________.

[ ] If it s the 20 bucks I owe you, forget it!

[ ] Where s the 20 bucks you owe me?

[ ] Who are you? Never heard of you.

Yours truly,

[His name]

### Request Unit of Assignment

To find out the unit and military installation a person is assigned to, write a letter to the appropriate locator, including as much identifying information as you have, and request his unit of assignment. Again, this can be accomplished very easily using the active duty military list on the Internet (see Chapter 5).

**Air Force —**

*Active Duty, Retired and Reserve:*
U.S. Air Force World-Wide Locator
AFPC-MSIMDL
550 C. Street West, Suite 50
Randolph AFB, TX 78150-4752
(210) 565-2248, (210) 652-5774 Recording
*www.afpc.af.mil*
($3.50 fee)

The Air Force Locator will forward only one letter per each request and will not provide overseas unit of assignment. Requests with more than one address per letter will be returned without action. Include a self-addressed stamped envelope with request for unit assignment. The locator will explain if the individual is separated from the Air Force. This locator has base assignment information on Air Force personnel since 1971. Include any former known base assignments when making your request.

**Army —**

*Active duty:*
World-Wide Locator
U.S. Army Enlisted Records
and Evaluation Center
8899 East 56th Street
Indianapolis, IN 46249-5301
(703) 325-3732
*www.erec.army.mil/wwl*

The Army locator furnishes military addresses for individuals currently serving on active duty in the Army and for the Department of the Army civilians. All requests must contain the individual's full name and the Social Security number or date of birth. No information will be given without one of the above identifying numbers. Their hours of operation are 7:30 a.m. to 4:00 p.m. eastern time. Written requests should be mailed to the above address with a check or money order in the amount of $3.50 for each name submitted made payable to "Finance Officer" (do not send cash). You should receive a reply in seven to ten working days.

This locator holds separation data for two years. Separation data includes date and place of separation.

For bonafide emergencies, call Total Army Personnel Command Staff Duty Officer at (703) 325-8851. This office has the microfiche of all individuals currently on active duty in the Army and all retired Army personnel. It is available 24 hours a day. You may also contact the American Red Cross through your local chapter listed in your phone book.

*Army: Retired from Active Duty, Reserve or Army National Guard:*

The Army Retired Locator is no longer operating. The best method to locate a retired Army member is to use Internet databases, computer searches, or the Defense Finance and Accounting Service.

You can track down Army National Guard members by contacting the State Adjutant's General Office in the appropriate state. Address your letter to the attention of the State Adjutant General. Refer to Appendix A for address and phone number.

**Coast Guard —**

The Coast Guard will provide ship or station of assignment and unit telephone number of active duty personnel.

*Active Duty:*
Commandant
(CGPC-ADM-3)
U.S. Coast Guard
2100 Second Street, S.W.
Washington, DC 20593-0001
(202) 267-1340, (202) 267-4985 Fax

*Retired:*
Commanding Officer (RAS)
U.S. Coast Guard Pay and Personnel Center
444 S.E. Quincy Street
Topeka, KS 66683-3591
(785) 357-3415, (785) 295-2639 Fax
(no fee)

*Reserve:*
Commandant
U.S. Coast Guard
2100 2nd Street, S.W.
Washington, DC 20593-0001
(202) 267-0547
(202) 267-4310 Fax
($3.50 fee)

**Marine Corps —**

*Active Duty and Marine Corps Selected Reserve:*
U.S. Marine Corps-CMC
(MMSB-10)
2008 Elliot Road, Room 201
Quantico, VA 22134-5030
(703) 784-3942, (703) 784-5792 Fax
($3.50 fee)

*Retired from active duty or Marine Corps Reserve:*
HQ U.S. Marine Corps
Manpower & Reserve Affairs (MMSR-6)
3280 Russell Road
Quantico, VA 22134-5103
(703) 784-9310, (703) 784-9434 Fax
(no fee)

**Navy —**

*Active Duty and Reserve:*
Department of Navy
Navy Personnel Command
PERS-312
5720 Integrity Drive
Millington, TN 38055-3120
(901) 874-3388, (901) 874-2660 Fax
($3.50 fee)

*Retired and Navy Individual Ready Reserve (IRR), Inactive Reserve:*
Commanding Officer (N3)
Naval Reserve Personnel Center
4400 Dauphine Street
New Orleans, LA 70149-7800
($3.50 fee; don't put return address on letter to be forwarded.)

If a locator is unable to identify the person you are looking for, contact the appropriate Defense Finance and Accounting Office. These centers maintain files of all retired military members (active duty, reserve and National Guard) and Survivor Benefit Plan annuitants (widows, widowers and some dependent children). They can reveal to third parties the names and rank/pay grade of retired members and annuitants and will forward letters to the retired members/annuitants in the same manner as the regular locators. The Social Security number and name, or name and date of birth are usually required. No fee is charged.

*Retired Pay Accounts.* Retired Pay Center for Army, Air Force, Navy and Marine Corps:

Defense Finance and Accounting Services
PO Box 99191
Cleveland, OH 44199-1126
(800) 321-1080, (216) 522-5955
(800) 469-6659 Fax

*Survivor Benefit Plan Annuitants:* For Army, Air Force, Navy and Marine Corps:

Defense Finance and Accounting Services
6760 E. Irvington Place
Denver, CO 80279-6000
(800) 435-3396, (303) 676-6552
(800) 982-8459 Fax

Coast Guard Retired:
Human Resources and Information Center
Retiree and Annuitant Services
444 S.E. Quincy Street
Topeka, KS 66683-3591
(800) 772-8724, (785) 295-2639 Fax

## Veterans

By definition, a veteran is a person who has served on active duty in one or more of the armed forces. Individuals who have served only in the reserves or National Guard are not considered veterans.

There are a lot of resources to help you locate a particular veteran: the Department of Veterans Affairs, National Personnel Records Center, veterans organizations, military reunion organizations or private organizations.

### Department of Veterans Affairs (VA)

The Department of Veterans Affairs (formerly the Veterans Administration) is very cooperative in providing assistance in locating veterans. There are more than 25 million living veterans.

The VA does not have addresses of all veterans listed in its records. The files only list the addresses of people who have, at some time, applied for VA benefits such as education assistance, disability compensation, pensions, home loans, and VA insurance. They will list the most recent address they have—usually the place where he lived the last time he corresponded with the agency. Since 1974 the VA has the name and Social Security number of everyone discharged from all branches of the armed forces. But they don't have an address unless the person makes a claim.

In some cases it's possible to obtain a veteran's Social Security number from the VA if he applied for benefits after April 1973. Write a letter to the VA and request the veteran's VA claim number. Provide the veteran's name, service number or date of birth. Include check for $2 payable to the "Department of Veterans Affairs." If the number returned starts with "C" followed by nine digits then the VA claim number is also the person's Social Security number. Mail to:

VA Records Processing Center
PO Box 5020
St. Louis, MO 63115 (314) 538-4500

The VA will forward a letter in the same manner as the armed forces. Before you give it a try, give them a call at (800) 827-1000. It will magically connect you with your nearest VA Regional Office. Although they won't give you an address over the phone, they will verify that a file exists. Explain to the VA counselor that you wish to verify that a veteran is listed in their files and ask if they have a current address. Give the person's full name and service number, Social Security number or VA file or claim number, if you know it. If you don't have this information the VA can sometimes identify veterans with either a date of birth, city and state from which he entered the service, branch of service, middle name or, possibly the name alone, if it's unique. If he's listed, ask for his claim number.

To forward a letter, place your correspondence in an unsealed, stamped envelope without your return address. Put the veteran's name and VA claim number on the front of the envelope. Next prepare a short fact sheet and explain that you request that the VA forward this letter to the veteran. Tell them the nice folks at their Regional Office gave you the VA claim number. Also include any other pertinent information that might help them identify him.

If they can't identify him, they'll return your letter to you. They will also inform you if the Postal Service can't deliver it for some reason. Mail your request to:

VA Records Processing Center
PO Box 5020
St. Louis, MO 63115

**Veterans Associations**

Another important resource for locating veterans is veterans associations. They will not give out addresses of their members, but will forward a letter. We've scored many times going this route. Here's a short list of some of the largest veterans associations:

The American Legion
PO Box 1055
Indianapolis, IN 46206
(2,900,000 members)
(317) 630-1200, (317) 630-1241 Fax
*www.legion.org*

Disabled American Veterans
National Headquarters
PO Box 14301
Cincinnati, OH 45250-0301
(1,000,000 members)
(606) 441-7300, (606) 441-2088 Fax
*www.dav.org*

The Retired Officer's Association
201 N. Washington Street
Alexandria, VA 22314-2539
(400,000 members)
(703) 549-2311, (703) 838-8173 Fax
*www.troa.org*

Veterans of Foreign Wars of the U.S.
406 W. 34th Street, Suite 523
Kansas City, MO 64111
(2,000,000 members; two names per request.)
(816) 756-3390, (816) 968-1157 Fax
*www.vfw.org*

Vietnam Veterans of America, Inc.
1224 "M" street, NW
Washington, DC 20005
(202) 628-2700, (202) 628-5880 Fax
*www.vva.org*

Non-Commissioned Officers Assn.
10635 IH 35 North
San Antonio, TX 78233
(150,000 members)
(210) 653-6161
*www.ncoausa.org*

Veterans of the Vietnam War, Inc.
760 Jumper Road
Wilkes-Barre, PA 18702-8033
(717) 825-7215
(717) 825-8223 Fax
*www.vvnw.org*

**Women Veterans**

Locating women veterans can be particularly frustrating because many get married and change their last names. Her phone number and other information is often listed under her married name. Even if her husband passes away, she may leave the phone listing in her late husband's name. However, some information is available if you have certain identifying information: maiden name, branch of service, approximate age, years she served in the military and her hometown.

Use most of the same procedures when looking for women veterans. Check with the Department of Veterans Affairs, perform the applicable computer searches (see Chapters 4 and 5), check with the active duty, reserve and retired locators, also check with one of the many veterans associations, such as VFW, American Legion, or AMVETS. Don't forget to check the officer registers (see page 137). Try checking with some of these veterans associations that list their members by maiden name and hometown:

Women in Military Service for America
5510 Columbia Pike Street #302
Arlington, VA 22204
(800) 222-2294, (703) 533-1155
(703) 931-4208 Fax
*www.wimsa.org*

Vietnam Women's Memorial Project, Inc.
2001 "S" Street, N.W., Suite 302
Washington, DC 20009
(202) 328-7253, (202) 986-3636 Fax

WAVES National
444 Moore Road
Pine Mountain, GA 31822
(706) 663-8253

Women's Army Corps Veterans Assn.
PO Box 5577
Fort McClellan, AL 36205
(205) 820-4019

## Military Records

### National Personnel Records Center

The NPRC is a branch of the National Archives and Records Administration. When a servicemember is discharged, retires or passes away, they send his military personnel file to the NPRC in St. Louis, Missouri. There are approximately 60 million records deposited there.

In certain situations, the people at the NPRC will forward correspondence to the last known address of a veteran. They put his address into his military personnel file when he separates from active duty, when his reserve commitment is completed or if he writes to the center after his discharge. They'll forward a letter to him, usually at no charge, if or when:

- They need to contact him regarding VA or Social Security benefits.
- Veteran will have veterans benefits affected.
- Veteran may have fathered illegitimate children.
- Forwarding is in the best interest of the veteran or next of kin—such as an estate settlement.
- Someone is making a legitimate effort to collect a debt.

A search fee of $3.50 is applicable only when the forwarding of correspondence is not in the veteran's interest, e.g., debt collect. Make checks payable to "Treasurer of the United States."

The NPRC will place the letter to be forwarded in another envelope and will add the individual's name and last known address. In the event the letter is not delivered, it will go back to the NPRC, but no one will tell you. Contact:

National Personnel Records Center
9700 Page Boulevard
St. Louis, MO 63132

**Military Personnel Records (201 File)**

There's a lot of great information in a former serviceman's military personnel file. Most important is probably his date of birth, but there are a lot of other clues in the file. You can send a letter to the NPRC and, if you have enough identifying information, the people there will send you "releasable information"—certain information is blacked out.

If someone was in the military, his file is available to anyone. You can request the files of President Kennedy, Elvis Presley, Ross Perrot, Audie Murphy—anyone. If the file is there, you can order it. But you must request it citing the "Freedom of Information Act." See Appendix C for a sample letter.

When you get the file you're apt to learn the veteran's rank/grade, complete legal name, duty status, date of rank, service number, date of birth, dependents (including name, sex and age), gross salary, geographical location of duty assignments, future assignments (approved), unit or office telephone number, source of commission (officers), military and civilian education level, promotion sequence number, awards and decorations, official photography, record of court-martial trials (unless classified), city/town/state of last known residence, date of that address, places of induction and separation, place of birth, date and location of death, and place of burial, if he's passed away.

Because of recent changes to the Freedom of Information Act regulations, the armed forces may not provide date of birth, official photo, records of court martial of members on active duty or in the reserves or National Guard. The National Personnel Records Center, however, will provide those items. The Privacy Act prevents you from getting your hands on his medical information, Social Security number or present address.

A Standard Form 180 (SF 180) should be used to request this information. This form can be found in Appendix C of this book or at *www.nara.gov.*

**Requesting Unit or Ship Rosters**

Yes, these are the all-important unit rosters that we talked about in the beginning of this chapter—the document that saved the day for many of our cases. Remember, the unit or ship roster (muster roll) is a list of personnel who were assigned to a particular unit or ship at a certain time period—be very specific; give month and year.

The first thing you must know to acquire this document is the unit or ship your person was assigned to. If you don't know then we suggest calling a military historian and ask if they know someone who might have that information.

Okay, now you have the name of the unit or ship. Who do you send it to, and how long does it take to get the roster back? Send your request to the National Personnel Records Center (NPRC), 9700 Page Boulevard, St. Louis, MO 63132. You can request these documents citing the FOIA and not have to pay a fee; otherwise it can run you about $15 per hour. The NPRC receives over 200,000 requests for records per month, so it can take several months for you to finally get your order.

**Veterans Who Have Passed Away**

It's a sad reality that the person you're looking for may have passed away. There are many ways to find out. If the person is indeed a veteran, the VA is the place to start. The people there will tell you over the telephone if they have a report of death for a veteran. If so, they'll also give out other important information—date of birth, branch of service and service number. Don't forget about using the Social Security Master Death Index on the Internet or at your local library.

Each military service has a casualty branch. They can provide copies of casualty reports or certain information on people who died on active duty or in retired status.

*Air Force*
HQ AFPC/DPWCS
550 "C" Street West, Suite 14
Randolph AFB, TX 78150-6001
(210) 652-5514

*Army*
Army Casualty & Memorial Affairs Operation Center
Total Army Personnel Command
TAPC-PED
2461 Eisenhower Avenue
Alexandria, VA 22331-0482
(703) 325-5300

*Marine Corps*
Headquarters, U.S. Marine Corps
Manpower & Reserve Affairs, MRC
3280 Russell Road
Quantico, VA 22134-5103
(703) 784-9512, (703) 784-9823 Fax
*WWII to present.

*Navy*
Navy Personnel Command, NPC-621
Casualty Assistance Branch
Millington, TN 38055-6210
(800) 368-3202
*WWII to present.

*Coast Guard*
Commandant (HSC)
U.S. Coast Guard
2100 2nd Street, S.W.
Washington, DC 20593

Remember, if you have not heard from your friend or relative for many years, or if he's up in years and you've struck out everywhere else, you might have to consider the reality that he may no longer be living.

## American Battle Monuments Commission

The American Battle Monuments Commission can provide the names of 124,912 U.S. war dead of WWI and WWII who are interred in American burial grounds in foreign countries. They can provide the names of 94,093 U.S. servicemen and women who were missing in action or lost or buried at sea during WWI, WWII, the Korean and Vietnam Wars.

American Battle Monuments Commission
Courthouse Plaza II, Suite 500
2300 Clarendon Blvd.
Arlington, VA 22201
(703) 696-6900, (703) 696-6666 Fax
*www.abmc.org*

We recently took on a very difficult case. A woman who was born in 1944 wanted to find her birth father. The only information she knew was that her father's name was John Burn, that he would be about 83 years old, and he was in the Army stationed in Illinois in 1943 and 1944. It was impossible to find the correct John Burn using the telephone directory so we tried running a date of birth computer search. Nothing. Then we checked Social Security Master Death Index and two men named John Burn, both the right age popped up. Both, however, had died in Illinois. So we called the VA to determine if they had any information on the two dead men. They did. One had been in the Navy and the other the Army. So we asked for all information about the Burn who had been in the Army—specifically his service number and place of death. This information allowed us to request copies of his military records to find out if there were any other children. The obituary also provided information about his children. Our client wasn't able to meet her father, but at least she learned about his military career and found out she had a half brother and sister.

## Selective Service Commission

The classification records of everyone who registered for the draft under the Selective Service Act are open for public inspection. So are the agency's information ledgers. These classification records list name, date of birth, draft classification, date to report for induction, and in some cases, date of separation. Records were maintained from 1940 to 1975 and are at various Federal Record Centers (see Appendix B). County records are also available in some main libraries. For more information contact:

National Headquarters
Selective Service System
1515 Wilson Blvd, 4th Floor
Arlington, VA 22209-2425
(703) 605-4100, (703) 605-4106 Fax
*www.sss.gov*

*Military Officers Registers* are excellent resources for gathering information on people who served as officers and warrant officers in the armed forces. Each year, every branch of the service published a *Register* of regular, reserve and retired officers. Earlier editions contain name, rank, service number, date of birth, colleges and universities attended, and some assignment information. Later editions (1968–1980) list name, rank, Social Security number, date of birth and other miscellaneous service data. The Privacy Act put an end to the *Registers* in 1981, although some copies are available on microfiche. Try obtaining copies of these *Registers* through your local library's inter-library loan program, military libraries or military academy libraries.

*U.S. Air Force Register* was an annual list of active and retired personnel. It includes service number (pre mid-1969) or Social Security number, and date of birth.

*The U.S. Army Register* came out yearly and contains lists of active, reserve and retired officers. It lists service number (pre mid-1969) or Social Security number, and date of birth. Before 1969 active lists included the state of birth and any military training.

*Register of Commissioned and Warrant Officers—Navy and Marine Corps and Reserve Officers on Active Duty—of the United States Naval Reserve* and *Register of Retired Com-*

*missioned and Warrant Officers, Regular and Reserve of the United States Navy and Marine Corps* were annual lists that included service number (pre-1972) or Social Security number, and date of birth.

*Register of Officers (Coast Guard)*. Published annually. Lists officers and warrant officers with date of birth and service number. Later editions include cadets at the U.S. Coast Guard Academy and social security numbers.

## Directories of Alumni of the Military Academies

*Register of Graduates of the United States Air Force Academy.* This book has begun to appear in a "condensed" version. The 1989 *Register* is the most recent "complete" version. It contains date of birth; full biographical sketches listing awards, decorations and special honors. Spouse's name and notations indicating most recently known place of employment may appear. Rank, reserve status, year and circumstance of leaving service also may be included. Names of deceased alumni appear in italics. The 1994 *Register* contains complete historical biographic information.

*Register of Graduates and Former Cadets of the United States Military Academy.* This book includes state and date of birth. Every effort has been made to include awards, separation date, rank, prior military service, colleges and degrees earned, current address and current employment. Deceased graduate's names are printed in italics.

*Register of Alumni: Graduates and Former Naval Cadets and Midshipmen.* This U.S. Naval Academy yearbook has date and place of birth, last known address, decorations, awards, special assignments, retirement, and rank attained. Marine Corps officers are designated. A letter "D" denotes deceased alumni. The name and address of the widow is listed, if available.

*Alumni Directory of the U.S. Coast Guard Academy.* Published annually. Includes name, address and class year. It does not contain biographical information such as date of birth.

## The National Archives

The National Archives and other federal agencies have casualty information. The following is a list of military computer records maintained by the National Archives. These records are available to the public in either computer formats or in printouts. In the near future, these database should be on various Internet military sites. See Appendix B.

*Korean Conflict Casualty File* contains data of all U.S. military personnel who died by hostile means in the Korean conflict. There are 32,642 records with names, service numbers and dates of death from 1950–1957.

*Southeast Asia Combat Area Casualties Database* contains 58,152 records of all U.S. military personnel who died as a result of hostilities or other causes in Cambodia, China, Laos, North Vietnam, South Vietnam or Thailand from 1957–1989.

*Korean War Casualty File, U.S. Army* contains 109,975 records of both fatal and nonfatal Army casualties.

*The Casualty Information System* for the periods 1961–1981 contains records of casualties suffered by all U.S. Army personnel and their dependents. Extracts of records of U.S. Army active duty personnel who have died are available.

You must put any and all requests for copies in writing and include payment. For fee information contact:

Center for Electronic Records (NSX)
National Archives and Records Administration
8601 Adelphi Road
College Park, MD 20740-6001
(301) 713-6630, (301) 713-6911 Fax
*www.nara.gov/nara/electronic/*

### Locate People in the Military Prison

Don't overlook the possibility your subject ended up in the slammer. You can find out if a former military member is or has been imprisoned in the U.S. Disciplinary Barracks (military prison) at Ft. Leavenworth, Kansas. Just call (913) 684-4743. Their current guest list includes some 1,500 inmates from all branches of the service. The prison keeps records of former inmates for up to ten years. The prison staff can search the files with a name only—the Social Security number and date of birth are not required. Their website is at *http://leav-www.army.mil/usdb/*.

# Other Resources

Most of this book is organized by "task"—such as adoption-related searching, background checking, finding someone who was in the military, or using the Internet. That's because the average reader has just one or two types of searches or tasks to accomplish, and zeroing in on those subjects wastes less time.

But such a method can't possibly include all the little bits of information that are out there. So we've created this chapter as a catch-all to make sure nothing slips between the cracks. When confronted with a difficult search, you can't have too much information.

Also, be sure to make good use of the index in the back of this book. It's designed to help you find subjects even if you don't have the exact name.

## FEDERAL GOVERNMENT SOURCES

No matter how far from the city some people decide to live—no matter how deep in the woods—it's unlikely they'll be able to avoid being listed with one federal agency or another. If they didn't work for an agency, maybe they collected money from it, paid money to it, served time in one of its facilities or were investigated by it. The point? Don't overlook the federal government connection.

As long as you don't make it look as if you're trying to invade someone's privacy or stalk them, most federal agencies will lend you a helping hand. At the very least they'll probably forward a letter to the person you're looking to find. Maybe they'll even confirm that they're paying benefits to the person or have issued some sort of license to him. Following are just some of the agencies you might approach for information or assistance in locating someone.

### National Archives and Records Administration

See Appendix B for information and addresses for NARA.

### Federal Information Center

Don't waste your time getting referred all over the place by calling the wrong federal agency. It can be confusing. Take, for example, the U.S. Postal Inspection Service. It neither inspects the mail nor works to improve service. But a lot of people still call that office when their mail arrives late, wasting everyone's time. Prevent spinning your wheels by first calling the Federal Information Center. This is a great resource for finding the locations of federal agencies—from the executive branch, to congressional offices to the federal courts and more. They'll listen to your problem and, in most cases, quickly name the agency you should be contacting and probably even give you the phone number or address. Phone them toll free at (800) 688-9889.

## Internal Revenue Service

The Internal Revenue Service will *forward letters* for humane reasons to people listed in their files who can be identified with a Social Security number. But they'll help only in cases of:

- An urgent or compelling nature, such as a serious illness.
- An imminent death or death of a close relative.
- A person seeking a missing relative.

A reunion or tracing a family tree does not qualify as a humane purpose.The Internal Revenue Service will not forward letters concerning debts.

If the IRS finds an address, they will put it in one of their envelopes and forward it to the person you're seeking. All they will tell you is that they forwarded the letter—they won't divulge the person's address or any tax information. It's up to the person you're looking for to contact you. If the IRS forwards a letter and the Postal Service can't deliver it, the IRS will destroy the letter without giving you any notification. Check the telephone book for the nearest IRS office.

By the way, if you lost track of your ex-spouse's Social Security number, just request the IRS to send you a copy of any of your old, joint tax returns. Check with your local IRS office for a request form.

## Social Security Administration

The Social Security Administration will sometimes *forward letters* (unsealed) to people whose names are listed in their files. This is only done for certain humanitarian reasons—reasons that are generally beneficial to the person receiving the letter—locating missing relatives, medical needs, locating heirs to estates, assisting people with claims, etc. If the agency likes the looks of your letter, it's staff will send it on to either the person's employer or directly to the person.

Before they offer any help, however, the Social Security Administration must determine that it's reasonable to assume the person being contacted would want to receive the letter and reply. This method has worked for a lot of people. Some have told us that the staffers there actually read the letter to make sure everything's on the up and up.

The Social Security Administration's guidelines include:

1. A strong compelling reason must exist, for example:
   a. A humanitarian purpose will be served (e.g., a close relative is seriously ill, is dying or died).
   b. A minor child is left without parental guidance.
   c. A defendant in a felony case seeks a defense witness.
   d. A parent wishes to locate a son or daughter.
   e. Consent of the missing person is needed in connection with an adoption proceeding for his/her child.

2. The missing person would want to know the contents of the letter.

3. The missing person's disappearance occurred recently enough that the Social Security Administration can reasonably expect to have a useable address.

4. All other possibilities for contacting the missing person have been exhausted.

**Forwarding Procedures**

Submit your request in writing to the Social Security Administration, giving the following information:

1. Missing person's name and Social Security number, if known.

2. If the Social Security number is not available, give other identifying information such as date and place of birth, name of parents, name and address of last known employer, and period of employment.

3. Reason for wanting to contact the person.

4. Last time seen.

5. Other contacts that have been exhausted.

Enclose your letter to the person in an unsealed, stamped envelope. The Social Security administration will try to find an address in their records for the person. If they find one, they'll forward your letter. They will notify you if they cannot forward a letter because they couldn't find a Social Security number. The SSA cannot tell you whether:

- They found an address for the person.
- They were able to forward a letter.

Here's a tip we can pass along. Folks who have succeeded using this method say they had a lot better luck working with the *local* Social Security Administration office than with a main office. One woman hadn't heard from her son in over 10 years. She took what information she had to the local office. The people there identified his file and forwarded her letter the same day.

**If Your Search Is Money-Related**

If your search is all about money, the people at the Social Security Administration are going to want some pretty compelling and convincing reasons before they'll forward your letter. And they're going to want to know that the person you're looking for is unaware of the money matters at hand. Here are some "for instances":

- The missing person is a beneficiary of an estate.
- He's entitled to some insurance proceeds.
- An important document is being held for him.

In these cases, follow the same procedures as we mentioned above, but include a personal check, cashier's check or money order in the amount of $3 per letter. Make it payable to "Social Security Administration." If they strike out, the Treasury Department will send you a refund. Here's a useful tip: When you make the payment, be sure to ask for a receipt. That way, if the person you're looking for has changed his name, the new name may show up on the receipt. Mail correspondence to:

Social Security Administration
Office of Central Records Operations
300 N. Green Street
Baltimore, MD 21201
(800) 772-1213

## U.S. Congressional Assistance

You should never have expectations of fast, efficient service from the military or the federal government. But if you've tried everything and still can't get them to budge, it may be time to call on the only federal employees who believe, even slightly, that they have to answer to you—your elected representatives in Congress. Just call or write your U.S. Senator or Representative. They want your vote, so they'll answer a lot quicker than others at the federal level—usually in less than two weeks.

Almost every federal agency has a "governmental relations" person or office in Washington DC whose sole job is to quickly solve problems brought to their attention by elected officials in Congress. Since every agency has a legislative committee pulling it's purse strings, they don't want to tick off Congress. The governmental relations people are authorized to quickly resolve just about any complaint or solve any problem. Write a letter—not more than a page or two in length—that outlines specifically what you're trying to accomplish, the specific problem you're experiencing, and a detailed description of what you've already done. Be sure to name names and provide phone numbers and addresses of people with whom you've had contact. If there is a valid urgency, be sure to tell them that. Even if the federal agency can't solve the problem, sometimes the Congressman's staff will go out of their way to help you. We receive a lot of inquiries from state and federal politicians on behalf of their constituents.

Your U.S. Senators and Representatives will be listed in your local telephone book. It never hurts to call the local office first. If the staff there can't help you, they may tell you the name of a specific staffer in Washington DC who can solve your problem. The telephone number for the U.S. Capitol in Washington is (202) 224-3121. Ask the operator for the office of your particular Senator or Representative. If you prefer to write to your Representative, the address is:

Honorable [name here]
United State House of Representatives
Washington, DC 20515

To write your Senator, the address is:

Honorable [name here]
United States Senate
Washington, DC 20510

## U.S. Postal Service

For many years, anyone could obtain a person's new address from the U.S. Postal Service by using the Freedom of Information Act—that is, if the person had submitted a change-of-address card. Unfortunately, they quit providing this information as of April, 1994. However, the U.S. Postal change-of-address file is still available to credit bureaus and professional searchers.

You may still be able to obtain a person's new address by mailing a letter to the last known address, and writing on the envelope "DO NOT FORWARD — ADDRESS CORRECTION REQUESTED." The post office will place a label on the envelope showing the new address and return your letter to you.

Try this method when you forward letters through the armed forces, world-wide locators, base locators, alumni associations and the Social Security Administration.

The Postal Service keeps change-of-address information for 18 months; they will forward letters for only 12 months.

Also try writing the postmaster where the person once lived (especially in small towns) in case he may have some additional information. Many small town postmasters have held their jobs for years and know the location or relatives of numerous people who once lived there.

## Office of Personnel Management

The Office of Personnel Management operates a centralized service that locates most federal civil service employees, except those employed by the judicial and congressional offices, the U.S. Postal Service, the Tennessee Valley Authority, the General Accounting Office, the FBI, and other intelligence agencies. Hard to believe there are any left, but there are. The only information they're allowed to release is the name and address of the person's employing agency, the location of his actual place of employment, or the address of the agency's personnel office. The employing agency may tell you exactly where he works, if their policy permits. To request a search, submit the person's name and Social Security number. It's going to take them a couple of weeks to reply, so don't just sit back and wait—turn to another part of this book and keep searching. Remember, there are always several onramps to any freeway.

U.S. Office of Personnel Management
1900 "E" Street, N.W.
Room 7494
Washington, DC 20415

Here are the numbers for some of the agencies the Office of Personnel Management doesn't track:

| | |
|---|---|
| U.S. Public Health Service | (301) 443-2403 |
| Central Intelligence Agency | (703) 613-8170 |
| Federal Bureau of Investigation | (202) 324-4164 |
| U.S. Postal Service | (202) 268-2000 |
| Government Accounting Office | (202) 512-5811 |
| Tennessee Valley Authority | (615) 632-2101 |
| Senate Employees | (202) 224-3207 |
| House of Representatives Employees | (202) 225-6514 |
| Employees of Federal Courts | (202) 273-2777 |
| National Oceanic and Atmospheric Administration | (800) 299-6622 |

It's also possible to find the local office of a civil service employee if you know for which agency the person works. Contact the local personnel office and ask for information.

### Library of Congress

If you are near the Library of Congress in Washington DC, you should, indeed, drop in and check out the information available there. We're talking about a collection of literally hundreds of thousands of books and reference materials that may be of assistance to you. Of most interest to searchers is the largest collection of city directories in the country. For more information you may contact the Library of Congress at (202) 707-5000.

### Federal Aviation Administration

The Federal Aviation Administration will provide a pilot's current address. You can have them search their files using a name only—that is, if the name is not too common. If it's fairly common, you may need the person's date of birth, Social Security number or the FAA pilot certificate number. Your request will show up in the pilot's FAA file. And if you know the state or states in which the person you're looking for may have resided or worked, the FAA may be able to find that he owns an airplane. That information will include a mailing address. It's all a matter of public record.

FAA Airmen Certification Branch
AVN-460
PO Box 25082
Oklahoma City, OK 73125
(405) 954-3261

*See Chapter 5 for a website listing people who are licensed by the FAA and/or own aircraft.

## Federal Publications (also see Appendix F)

The U.S. Government Printing Office sells numerous books published by the federal government—many that are valuable to searchers. Some include:

*U.S. Government Organization Manual* lists the address, telephone number and description of each federal agency and office.

*Directory of U.S. Government Depository Libraries* lists libraries that have federal publications.

*Where to Write for Vital Records* provides details on how to obtain birth, death, marriage and divorce records from each state.

Superintendent of Documents
U.S. Government Printing Office
Washington, DC 20402
(202) 512-1800

The Government Printing Office also maintains bookstores in some of the nation's larger cities. Call the number above for the bookstore nearest you.

*The National Zip Code Directory* is a publication of the U.S. Postal Service. It lists all cities in the U.S. with a post office, their zip codes, and the county where the city is located. Streets are listed for larger cities. You can buy this at any post office. Your library should also have a copy.

### Census Records

Census records can be used for finding older people or getting information on people known to have died (for example, for genealogies). U.S. censuses are taken every 10 years on years ending in zero, and the specific information is released to the public 70 years later. The latest census information available right now is from the 1920 census, and the 1930 census will be available in 2000. The censuses list names, ages, and occupations of all people (including children and infants) living in a household at the time the census was taken. Exact dates of birth are not given, only ages—for example, "9 years, 3 months." Census records on microfilm can be viewed at LDS Family History Centers and other genealogy libraries.

A few states and some major cities also conducted censuses, usually on years ending with five (1925, etc.).

### Is He in Federal Prison?

Are you looking for someone who might be in a federal prison? Call the U.S. federal prison locator at (202) 307-3126. They can check his name, and some aliases may be available. Most prison locators keep records of former inmates for up to ten years. Sometimes you can even locate him without his date of birth or Social Security number. If you think he may be in a state prison, refer to the phone numbers listed in Appendix A.

### Regional Government Depository Libraries

Every state has at least one Regional Government Depository Library. These libraries receive most of the new and revised government publications on a timely basis. These publications are then made available by loan to libraries that participate in an inter-loan program with the depository library.

Publications that can be obtained through this program include armed forces officers registers, Department of State employee registers, federal government telephone books, U.S. government pamphlets (census information, commercial laws, bankruptcy courts, federal tax matters, etc.). Ask your librarian how to request this service and what publications would be the most helpful for your search.

## NON-GOVERNMENTAL SOURCES

### The Salvation Army

The Salvation Army conducts searches of missing people through their national missing persons network. However, they only perform searches for immediate family members who have been missing for more than six months. There are four territorial headquarters that have missing persons services, as noted below. The seeking relative must contact the office that covers the state that the seeker resides in, not the state where the person being sought may be found. Ask for a registration form. A $25 fee is required.

The Salvation Army
Missing Persons Services
440 West Nyack Rd.
West Nyack, NY 10994
(800) 315-7699
*States and territories covered*: ME, VT, NH, MA, CT, RI, NY, NJ, DE, PA, OH, KY, PR, VI.

The Salvation Army
Missing Persons Services
1424 NE Expressway
Atlanta, GA 30329
(800) 939-2769
*States covered*: MD, WV, VA, KY, TN, NC, SC, GA, FL, MS, AL, AR, LA, OK, TX.

The Salvation Army
Missing Persons Services
2780 Lomita Blvd.
Torrance, CA 90505
(800) 698-7728
*States covered*: MT, WY, CO, NM, AZ, UT, NV, CA, OR, WA, AK, HI.

The Salvation Army
Missing Persons Services
10 W. Algonquin Rd.
Des Plaines, IL 60016
(847) 294-2000
*States covered*: MI, IN, IL, WI, MN, ND, SD, IA, MO, NE, KS.

## LDS Church Resources

The Family History Library of the LDS Church in Salt Lake City houses the most extensive collection of genealogical information in the world. Documents from around the world have been microfilmed and are available for inspection. The library is open every day except Sunday and holidays. It's information number is (801) 240-2331.

The LDS Church also has over 2000 "Family History Centers" located throughout the world. These Centers are small repositories that are linked to the main library in Salt Lake City and are available to the public. To find the center nearest you, look in your phone book under "Church of Jesus Christ of Latter Day Saints," then under that title look for "genealogy library" or "Family History Center." Or call the number listed below.

Church of Jesus Christ of Latter-Day Saints
Family History Department
35 North West Temple
Salt Lake City, UT 84150
(801) 240-2584

## Colleges, Universities and Alumni Associations

The Federal Family and Educational Rights and Privacy Act allows colleges and universities to release "directory information" to the public without consent of the student. However, a student may request that all or part of this information be withheld by making a written request to the admissions office. "Directory information" includes name, address, telephone listing, major, date and place of birth, dates of attendance, degrees and awards received and previous educational agencies or institutions attended. Some colleges may release a student's Social Security number. Also see Chapter 5 (Using the Internet) for more information on reaching colleges and universities.

Alumni associations keep track of former students to ask them for future donations. However, they normally will only forward a letter.

## American Red Cross

The American Red Cross assists people in locating family members in cases of emergency. If there is a bona fide emergency that involves active duty military, always contact the Red Cross first. The Red Cross is listed in your local telephone directory.

## Religious Affiliation

Religious affiliation should always be noted on the Individual Data Worksheet (see Chapter 2 and Appendix C) because it can be a great source of information. Write or call some of the churches of your subject's affiliation in the last town where he lived. They usually keep records of all their members. Talk with other members of the church or with the pastor/preacher/rabbi. They may remember your friend and have important information. Some churches also have death records of members.

Chapter 10

# Solving Difficult Cases

You've tried every trick in this book and you still can't find that person. What next? First of all, don't despair. It's just the nature of this business. The reality is, there is a small percentage of people who slip through the cracks of a conventional search and require a few extra steps.

Even the seasoned professional has a tough job finding certain people—the homeless, older or elderly folks residing in nursing homes or with family members, people living overseas or in prison, people who are intentionally trying to hide, and people who lost touch with friends and family members and died. Remember that people who are in these categories are usually not listed in most databases. Or if they are listed they may have a very old address. They may not have a credit history, they may not vote, they probably don't have a car and don't need a drivers license. They may not even have a telephone or a mailing address that shows up in the normal places. They're just not in the System. It would be hard to find these people using the normal computer searches and techniques we describe throughout this book. In this chapter we'll show you what extra steps you can take when you encounter problem searches.

## Homeless People

Street people are not included in the common databases we have discussed but there are sources out there. Think about the agencies and organization with whom the homeless interact. It's always a good idea to check with the Salvation Army (see Chapter 9) and other socially-related organizations that offer services to the needy. The local police and sheriff's department might have a record of the person you're seeking. It never hurts to ask. If they don't know the actual person you're looking for, they might very well know which organizations interact most with the homeless. Ask them if they've ever arrested your subject. Find out who the regular beat cops are in the areas where the homeless hang out. Check with local hospitals, free clinics, blood banks and government psychiatric facilities to see if they know the person. Don't forget the Department of Veterans Affairs hospitals if the person is a veteran. The VA facilities have separate databases of patients which are not the same as those kept by the VA Regional offices. Many churches provide meals and housing for homeless people.

Try posting notices at libraries, post offices and other spots around town describing the person you're looking for and give information on how they can contact you.

Another good resource is notifying homeless shelters across the country about the person you're seeking. There is a list of homeless shelters available on the Internet at *http://www.nmc.edu/~lanninl/us.htm*. Here's a sample listing:

Homeless Shelters in Arlington, TX:

(1) Arlington Night Shelter
Pete Pardes, Executive Director
325 W. Division Street
Arlington, TX 76011
Phone: (817) 548-9885
Fax: (817) 548-1609
E-mail: Not available
URL: Not Available

Summary of Services:

* Serves the Tarrant County area.
* Provides hot food, warm beds, education, and counseling for the homeless.
* Capacity: Up to 89 men, women and children each night.
* Five hours of educational classes each week are required of residents (from GED preparation to classes in ending domestic violence).
* Length of stay: Four weeks (an exception will be made if client has a job and is saving money toward a rent deposit—an additional five weeks).
* Staffed primarily by volunteers (only four full-time and seven part-time paid staff).

## The Elderly

Most elderly people have lived in the same place for a long time—certainly long enough for former neighbors to know what became of them. Every neighborhood has a resident busybody. Knock on a few doors and you're sure to zero in on him or her. There's a good chance you can get good leads from the local postal carrier, neighborhood retailers, gardeners, newspaper delivery people, local churches, senior citizen centers and even the local newspaper. Sadly, many older people who have an illness or trouble caring for themselves end up being warehoused in nursing homes or other long-term care facilities. Some live with family members—sometimes people who are distantly related. You may not know the names or addresses of your subject's children. But don't give up.

While many older people don't vote, don't have current credit information, don't have a drivers license and seldom have their own telephone number, there are still places where their names pop up. They may still own property. If not, they may have owned a home and sold it. Make contact with the local tax assessor and the recorder of deeds. You may find the names of people who bought the property. By looking at older tax rolls, you can also get the names and addresses of neighbors who may have known your subject, even if they've moved away. If you make a trip to the local court house, be sure to look in the civil index for probate files, conservatorships or even lawsuits by or against the person you're seeking.

When you're searching for an older person you should first check the Social Security Master Death Index or state and local vital statistics offices just to make sure he hasn't already died. It may seem a little morbid, but if the person you're seeking has died, you'll find out quicker this way and you'll surely save yourself a lot of time, energy and expense.

If he doesn't show up on the death index, and you've checked with your local Social Security office and they have no death listing under that name, ask the Social Security folks if he's receiving any type of benefits. And remember, in certain circumstances, the Social Security Administration will forward your letter to him. Go back and look at Chapter 9.

Investigative journalist Don Ray recalls the time he was searching for a very old man named George with a distinctive last name somewhere in the Los Angeles megalopolis and found only one listing for the last name.

"A young woman answered and said she had just married into the family the week before and didn't know any of the relatives," says Ray. "She said no one else was home. I asked her to search through the house for any lists of family members. She called me back in a few minutes and read to me from a family tree chart she had found in a drawer. It had the words 'Uncle George—dead?' written on one branch. She gave me the name of a man who appeared to be George's brother living in another California community. When I called that man, he told me he was sure his brother had died years ago, but gave me the most recent address—an address from more than twenty years earlier.

"I decided to drive to the address—it was an old residential hotel. I asked the desk clerk if he remembered George."

"'Sure I remember George,' the crusty old-timer told me. 'Hell, I had breakfast with him this morning. He should be up in his room—number 204.'"

Check local nursing homes—ask them if your subject is living there or did in the past. If the facility is a smaller one, they may tell you everything they remember about him. "Oh, Ralph left a year ago. His daughter moved to Michigan and she put him in a nice care facility close to her." Nursing homes are listed in the yellow pages of your phone book.

## People Living Overseas

It's not that hard to find a person living outside the United States. Most people moved overseas for work or to retire. The best sources of information are the U.S. State Department and the embassy of the country the person may be residing in. These offices are located in Washington, DC. Just check with directory assistance in Washington DC (202/555-1212) for their telephone numbers. You can also access a list of embassies on the Internet. See Chapter 5.

Most embassies have telephone books of people and businesses in their country. It's usually pretty easy to call directory assistance in a foreign country or city. Your local international operator can stay on the line to make sure you are communicating well with the foreign operators. Don't forget to use the same techniques you'd use in the U.S.—ask for the number of anyone with that last name. Call people with the same last name. There's a good chance they'll either know the family you're seeking or they may be able to read you more listings from their local directory than the international operator may be willing to give you.

Look for one of the CD-ROMs that list telephone numbers for most European countries. Check out the various international telephone directories and other great search engines on the Internet. Start with *http://www.albany.net/allinone*.See Chapter 5.

Consider contacting the company a person might be working for overseas. They should be able to forward a letter for you. Because of the Privacy Act, most companies and government agencies are reluctant to give out information about a person's whereabouts. The better you are on the phone with them, the better your chances of getting a clue. If the person works for a corporation, simply call the headquarters and ask them to send you their annual report. By law, they must send it if they are a publicly held corporation. The annual report will list the corporation's foreign offices and subsidiaries. City, county, state and federal agencies will usually give or sell you a copy of their agency's telephone directory. That can be a great resource for finding someone within the organization who will be more helpful.

### People Traveling Overseas

If you're trying to find someone who is traveling overseas try calling the State Department's Citizens Emergency Center at (202) 647-5225.

## Is He in Prison?

The United States has the largest percentage of incarcerated citizens of any country on earth. You might as well take a drive down that avenue—even if you'd rather not know. Your own gut feelings will tell you if there's a possibility he's in the slammer somewhere. City and county jails are required to let you know who's visiting their accommodations. The local court file will tell you who the probation officer is—or at least, which office handles him. The state corrections department will tell you if he's a current guest in any of their penal institutions. If your subject has already checked out, they'll probably tell you which parole office is in contact with your unfortunate friend. Also, check with the military prison at Ft. Leavenworth (913) 684-4629, or the federal prison locator at (202) 307-3126. They have information on current and former "guests."

## The I-Don't-Want-to-Be-Found Folks

People who are trying to hide are usually trying to avoid something—alimony, child support, debts or even prosecution. Most people in hiding share many of the same characteristics of deadbeat parents.

These guys are careful not to have any information about them in the computer databases—in particular, no listed telephone number. He could be living with a new girlfriend with her own phone listing. If he's serious about not being found, he's probably working at a job that pays him under the table—no credit, Social Security deductions or income tax returns to file. Maybe his girlfriend lets him buy things using her good credit. He probably won't be dumb enough to have a drivers license in his own name or showing his own address.

These are the hardest cases to solve. These guys move at the drop of a hat. They're modern-day vagabonds. There's always another city and another girlfriend to hide behind.

Keep in mind, however, that he may not be willing to shed his personal habits or vices. Check the local bars, bowling alleys, drag strips, truck stops, union halls and pool halls if he has ever shown any connection to these activities or jobs.

If the reason you're searching for someone is incredibly compelling or unusually visual, try teaming up with the news media. There are lots of programs that eat this stuff up. Drop a brief line to any of the following programs or call your local TV station to find out who produces such programs. If your story is full of human interest, you might be able to reach out to millions of people. Be creative, but honest.

Unsolved Mysteries
New Story Department
PO Box 10729
Burbank, CA 91510
*http://www.unsolved.com*

Other television shows such as Oprah, Montel, or Leeza, could also be helpful if they air some type of show about missing people or unsolved crimes.

Oprah
Harpo Productions
110 N. Carpenter St
Chicago, IL 60607-2146

Leeza
Paramount Domestic Television
5555 Melrose Avenue
Hollywood, CA 90038

Montel Williams
Viacom International, Inc.
433 W. 53rd St, 2nd Floor
New York, NY 10019

## Using Professional Searchers

You shouldn't need a professional searcher unless you've read this book through twice and exhausted every tip, lead, and resource we've provided. But if you should need to hire someone, make sure you check him out thoroughly. You can't imagine how many people out there have thrown away thousands of dollars on what should have been an hour-long search. We suggest calling at least five professionals. Tell them what you've already done and what you know about the person you're looking for. You'll quickly get a feel for who's trying to rip you off. You can check with private investigators, information brokers, specialized people-finders and even attorneys. Here's a place to start:

The National Association of Investigative Specialist is a worldwide network of private investigative professionals and/or agencies. With more than 1,500 members, it is one of the largest associations in the world for investigators.

National Association of Investigative Specialists
PO Box 33244
Austin, TX 78764
(512) 928-8190

Charles Eric Gordon is an attorney concentrating on locating persons who have been missing for a substantial period of time and/or about whom little information is known. He is a consultant to law firms, government agencies, private investigation firms and foreign governments in locating missing or absent witnesses, beneficiaries, heirs, debtors and other persons, but he does not consult on matters involving the location of birth parents, unless there is a court order.

Gordon has worldwide contacts and many years of experience in locating missing persons—experience gained in both private and governmental sectors. He often can assist in locating and acquiring information and public records that are generally difficult to access such as vital records, voter registration and court records (where legally available). He can also obtain, when necessary, copies of baptismal, cemetery and property records, some of which may be very old. For further information and fee charges please contact:

Charles Eric Gorden, Esq.
PO Box 514
Plainview, NY 11803-0514
(515) 433-5065

*Note*: Before using a professional investigator be sure to ask for references and make sure he or she is licensed in the necessary state. Also make sure you both agree what services are to be performed for a set price. Do not enter into an agreement for an hourly fee for a very difficult case. The fees could be enormous. If you've already paid someone for computer searches, don't pay to have the same search run again. Give all the information you've already obtained to the new professional investigator.

Another word of caution. Be sure you ask any professional researcher if they are using any illegal resources. An honest investigator will not be offended. With the increased use of computers and modems, there is a thriving black market out there for illegally obtained information from the Social Security Administration (current employment information), the FBI (criminal history sheets), the IRS (personal income tax information) and other local, state and federal agencies. You, the customer, are more likely to end up in jail than the person who sold you the tainted information. The trend has been that the information broker has been able to cut a deal with prosecutors to name the government source and the end-user, in trade for immunity. Don't get caught up in this nightmare.

## Closing Statement

We have certainly enjoyed teaching you about how to find people who are important to you. Hopefully your search will result in finding that person for a joyous reunion, meeting a family member for the first time or reuniting with friends and family. We hope that we have explained a sometimes difficult subject clearly and thoughtfully, so you can begin searching for just about anyone, using the techniques and methods we have included in this book.

Due to the number of resources we included, some of this information may change. We go to every effort to verify this information before press. If you have any questions or comments or are having unusual trouble with your search, please write to us at:

MIE Publishing
PO Box 17118
Spartanburg, SC 29301
E-mail: information@militaryusa.com

*—Debra Johnson Knox*

# Appendix A

## *State Offices & Other Information*

This directory is a listing of helpful information by state. It's meant to save you time, money, and hopefully a little aggravation. Most listings are official state offices but some are not—for example, some historical and genealogical societies are not part of the state government. The same goes for adoption researchers and adoption support groups. VA Regional Offices are listed here rather than at the federal level because they exist in each state. Anything listed in *italics* is informational or a heading and not part of the name or address.

Below is a listing and description of the categories and offices found under each state.

### Area Codes for Each State

Many new area codes have been put into use lately. If you have an old phone number, it may very well have a new area code. A telephone operator can help you. To find an area code for a particular town or city, simply ask the operator.

### State Government Information Number

This is the information operator for all state offices and agencies. Say you are looking for your old boyfriend who just happens to be a Certified Public Accountant in Oklahoma. Call the state government information operator and request the licensing office for CPAs. Then call that office to get his address and phone number.

### State Prison Locator

If you think someone's been in trouble with the law this may be a good place to start. Check with the prison locators to find out if your subject is residing in, or has been in, their facilities in the past ten years. They can search by legal name and alias. For federal prison information, see pp. 78 & 151.

### State Child Support Enforcement Office

This state office is a last resort when trying to collect child support. They help to locate people responsible for paying court-ordered child support. It's not recommended to contact this office first, but rather to work with your local county office. If your local office can't find your ex, then ask them to contact the state office or call them directly. These agencies can acquire addresses from federal agencies such as the Social Security Administration, Internal Revenue Service, Armed Forces and Office of Personnel Management.

### State Vital Statistics

Vital statistics offices maintain records of births, deaths, marriages, divorces and annulments. Often this information is maintained on centralized files, but must be searched manually. Only a few states have centralized computer files. Florida and California have computerized state death indexes. Each state determines what information can be released and the information may be limited to family members.

### State Drivers License Office

Some states will give out information contained in drivers license files while other states restrict the address portion. California and Hawaii do not release any information. In other states it may be available to family members only. Each state makes these determinations. Contact the state drivers license office to find out.

Drivers license records contain driver license number, expiration date, legal name, current address, and physical description. This also applies to identification cards.

### State Vehicle Titles & Registrations

State vehicle registration files are open to everyone except in a few states. These files give the name and address of owners of all motor vehicles that are registered in that particular state. Remember, motor vehicles include cars, motorcycles, trucks, trailers, RVs, and commercial vehicles.

### State Archives, Genealogical/Historical Societies

These offices can help in any search, especially a particularly difficult case. Their employees are trained searchers and can access many historical and genealogical records. Types of documents include old photographs, family history information, state military records, state census records, birth and death announcements, etc. These resources vary by state.

### Adoption Support Group/Researchers

Curry Wolfe publishes the *Blue Book* and was gracious to give us listings of adoption contacts. Her book lists all researchers and support groups by state. We tried to list at least one adoption support group and one adoption researcher for each state, but some states do not have a listing. If this is the case, we suggest you contact a researcher in a nearby state or one of the adoption organizations on pp. 100–101. For more adoption support groups, resources or researchers, try: *http://members.tripod.com/~win94/search.html.*

### State Adjutant General's Office

This is the top military office for a state. It's in charge of state Army and Air National Guard, and maintains records of people who are serving or have served in these groups.

### Veterans Affairs (VA) Regional Office

If you're looking for a military veteran, always check with your local VA Regional Office and ask if they have any information on your subject. Do they have him listed in their files? If so, do they have a current address? (If they do, they will only forward a letter.) Do they have a report of death? All VA Regional Offices are reached through the same 800 number.

When calling any office for help, hopefully whoever answers the phone will be polite and cooperative, but if this is not the case, call back. Someone else may answer. Then start over asking the same questions.

## ALABAMA

Area codes for state: 205, 256, 334
State government information number: (334) 242-8000
State prison locator: (334) 240-9500
State website: *www.state.al.us*

Child Support Enforcement Office
Gordon Persons Building
50 Ripley Street
Montgomery, AL 36130-1808
(800) 284-4347, (334) 242-9300
(334) 242-0606 Fax

*State Vital Statistics:*
Department of Public Health
Bureau of Vital Statistics
PO Box 5625
Montgomery, AL 36103
(334) 261-5033
*Divorce decrees are county records.

*State Driver Licenses:*
DPS, Driver License Division
PO Box 1471
Montgomery, AL 36102
(334) 242-9000

*State Vehicle Titles/Registrations:*
Motor Vehicle Division
Title/Registration Section
PO Box 327640
Montgomery, AL 36132
(334) 242-9000

*State Archives:*
Archives & History Department
Reference Rm, PO Box 300100
Montgomery, AL 36130-0100
(334) 242-4435
(334) 240-3433 Fax

Alabama Historical Association
PO Box 870380
Tuscaloosa, AL 35487-0380

Alabama Historical Commission
PO Box 300900
Montgomery, AL 36130-0900
(334) 242-3184

Alabama Genealogical Society
800 Lakeshore Drive
Birmingham, AL 35229
(205) 870-2749

Southern Society of Genealogists
Stewart University
PO Box 295
Centre, AL 35960
(205) 447-2939

*Adoption Support Group:*
Orphan Voyage
Attn: Leah Wesolowski
95 Indian Creek Rd #132
Huntsville, AL 35806
(205) 722-0506
E-mail: rfsmo8f@prodigy.com

*Adoption Researcher:*
Lynn Davis
196 Clara Street
Webb, AL 36376
(334) 794-7884

State Adjutant General
PO Box 3711
Montgomery, AL 36109-0711
(334) 271-7259

VA Regional Office
345 Perry Hill Road
Montgomery, AL 36109
(800) 827-1000

## ALASKA

Area code for state: 907
State government information number: (907) 465-2111
State prison locator: (907) 465-3376
State website: *www.state.ak.us*

*Child Support Enforcement Office:*
Alaska Department of Revenue
Child Support Enforcement
550 West 7th Avenue, Suite 310
Anchorage, AK 99501-6699
(907) 269-6900, (907) 269-6914
(800) 478-9900
E-mail:
Glenda_Straube@revenue.state.ak.us

*State Vital Statistics:*
Department of Health & Social Services
Bureau of Vital Statistics
PO Box 110675
Juneau, AK 99811-0675
(907) 465-3392

*State Driver Licenses:*
DMV, Drivers Records
PO Box 20020
Juneau, AK 99802
(907) 465-4335

*State Vehicle Titles/Registrations:*
Department of Motor Vehicles
ATTN: Research
2150 E. Dowling Road
Anchorage, AK 99507
(907) 563-5589

Adjutant General
PO Box 5800
Ft. Richardson, AK 99505-5800
(907) 428-6400

*State Archives:*
Alaska State Archives
141 Willoughby Avenue
Juneau, AK 99801-1720
(907) 465-2270
(907) 465-2270 Fax
E-mail: archives@eed.state.ak.us

Alaska Association for Historic Preservation
524 W. 4th Ave, Suite 203
Anchorage, AK 99501
(907) 272-2119

Alaska Historical Society
PO Box 100299
Anchorage, AK 99510-0299
(907) 276-1596

Alaska Genealogical Society
7030 Dickerson Drive
Anchorage, AK 99504

*Adoption Support Group:*
CUB
Jana Tackett
7105 Shorreson
Anchorage, AK 99504
(907) 333-2272

VA Regional Office
2925 DeBarr Road
Anchorage, AK 99508-2989
(800) 827-1000

## ARIZONA

Area codes for state: 480, 520, 602, 623
State government information number: (602) 542-4900
State prison locator: (602) 542-5586 or (900) 226-8682 (fee per minute)
State website: *www.state.az.us*

*Child Support Enforcement Office:*
Arizona Child Support Enforcement
PO Box 40458
Phoenix, AZ 85067
(602) 252-4045, (602) 248-3126 Fax

*State Vital Statistics:*
Department of Health Services
Vital Records Section
2727 West Glendale
Phoenix, AZ 85030
(602) 255-3260
*Divorce decrees are county records.

*State Driver Licenses/ Vehicle Titles/Registrations:*
Motor Vehicles Division
Records Services Section
Box 2100, Mail Drop 504M
Phoenix, AZ 85001
(602) 255-0072
*Same address for driving records and title/registration.

*State Archives:*
Library, Archives & Pub. Records Dept
State Capitol, Suite 342
1700 West Washington
Phoenix, AZ 85007
(602) 542-4159, (602) 542-4402 Fax
E-mail: archive@lib.az.us

Arizona Historical Society
949 East Second Street
Tuscon, AZ 85719
(602) 628-5774

State Historical Society
N. Fort Valley Rd, Rt. 4, Box 705
Flagstaff, AZ 86001
(602) 774-6272

State Historical Society
Yuma Branch
Century House Museum
240 South Madison Avenue
Yuma, AZ 85364
(602) 782-1841

State Genealogical Society
Arizona Society of Genealogists
6565 East Grant Road
Tuscon, AZ 85715

Arizona State Genealogical Society
PO Box 42075
Tuscon, AZ 85733-2075

Family History Society of Arizona
PO Box 310
Glendale, AZ 85311
(602) 926-1815

Genealogical Society of Arizona
PO Box 27237
Tempe, AZ 85282

*Adoption Support Group:*
Adult Adoptees Support Group
Dee Davis
7757 E. Marquise Drive
Tucson, AZ 85715
(520) 885-6771
E-mail: gnun24d@prodigy.com

*Adoption Researcher:*
Past, Present, Future
Sherri Ervin
7290 W. Shaw Butte Drive
Peoria, AZ 85345
(602) 486-3042
E-mail: azsherri@aol.com

State Adjutant General
5636 E. McDowell Road
Phoenix, AZ 65008-3495
(802) 267-2700

VA Regional Office
3225 N. Central Avenue
Phoenix, AZ 85012
(800) 827-1000

## ARKANSAS

Area code for state: 501, 870
State government information number: (501) 682-3000
State prison locator: (870) 267-6999
State website: *www.state.ar.us*

Child Support Enforcement
PO Box 8133
Little Rock, AR 72203
(800) 264-2445, (501) 682-8398
(501) 682-6002 Fax
E-mail: admin.ed.baskin@state.ar.us

*State Vital Statistics:*
Arkansas Department of Health
Division of Vital Records, Slot 44
4815 W. Markham Street
Little Rock, AR 72205-3867
(501) 661-2726
*Divorce decrees are county records.

*State Driver Licenses:*
Department of Driver Services
Driver Records Division
PO Box 1272, Room 127
Little Rock, AR 72203
(501) 682-7207

*State Vehicle Titles/Registrations:*
Office of Motor Vehicles
IRP Unit
PO Box 1272, Room 106
Little Rock, AR 72203
(501) 682-3333

*State Archives:*
Arkansas Historical Commission
One Capitol Mall
Little Rock, AR 72201
(501) 682-6900

Arkansas Historical Assn
University of Arkansas
Fayetteville, AR 72701
(501) 575-5884

Arkansas Historical Society
422 South Sixth Street
Van Buren, AR 72956

Arkansas Genealogical Society
1411 Shady Grove Road
Hot Springs, AR 71901
(501) 262-4513 Phone/Fax

*Adoption Researcher:*
Clorinda Arace
8809 Cloverhill Rd.
Little Rock, AR 72205
(501) 225-2379

State Adjutant General
Camp Robinson
N. Little Rock, AR 72199-9600
(501) 212-4001

VA Regional Office
PO Box 1280
N. Little Rock, AR 72115
(800) 827-1000

## CALIFORNIA

Area codes for state: 209, 213, 310, 323, 408, 415, 424, 510, 530, 559, 562, 619, 626, 650, 661, 669, 707, 714, 760, 805, 818, 831, 858, 909, 916, 925, 949
State government information number: (916) 657-9900
State prison locator: (916) 445-6713
State website: *www.state.ca.us*

*Child Support Enforcement Office:*
Department of Social Services
Child Support Bureau
744 "P" Street
Sacramento, CA 95814
(800) 952-4253, (916) 654-1556
(916) 653-8690 Fax

*State Vital Statistics:*
Dept. of Health Services
Office of Vital Records
PO Box 730241
Sacramento, CA 94244-0241
(916) 445-2684
*Divorce decrees are county records.

*Driver Licenses/Titles/Registrations:*
Department of Motor Vehicles
Information Request Counter
Box 944231, Mail Station C-198
Sacramento, CA 94244
(916) 657-8098

*State Archives:*
California State Archives
1020 "O" Street
Sacramento, CA 95814
(916) 653-7715, (916) 653-1734 Fax

Council for Promotion of History
California History Center
DeAnza College
21250 Stevens Creek Boulevard
Cupertino, CA 95014

California Historical Society
2099 Pacific Avenue
San Francisco, CA 94109-2235

California Genealogical Alliance
4808 East Garland Street
Anaheim, CA 92807-1005
(714) 777-0483

Professional Genealogists of Calif.
5048 J Parkway
Sacramento, CA 95823

*Adoption Support Group:*
Adoptee/Birthparent Connection
Tina Peddie
1365 Lesley Court
Santa Maria, CA 93454
(805) 922-4313, (805) 346-1156 Fax
E-mail: 72103,2257@compuserve.com

*Adoption Researcher:*
Curry Wolfe
PO Box 230643
Encinitas, CA 92023

*Adoption Researcher:*
Mary Lou Kozub
2027 Finch Ct
Simi Valley, CA 93063
(805) 583-4306, (805) 583-4160 Fax
E-mail: smvt47a@prodigy.com

State Adjutant General
PO Box 269101
Sacramento, CA 95826-9101
(916) 854-3310

VA Regional Office
8810 Rio San Diego Dr.
San Diego, CA 92108
(800) 827-1000

VA Regional Office
1301 Clay Street
Oakland, CA 94612
(800) 827-1000

## COLORADO

Area codes for state: 303, 719, 720, 970
State government information number: (303) 866-5000
State prison locator: (719) 579-9580
State website: *www.state.co.us*

Child Support Enforcement Office
Division of Human Services
1575 Sherman Street, 2nd Floor
Denver, CO 80203-1714
(303) 866-5994, (303) 266-2214 Fax

*State Vital Statistics:*
Colorado Department of Health
Vital Records Office
4300 Cherry Creek Drive, South
Denver, CO 80246-1530
(303) 692-2224
*Divorce decrees are county records.

*State Driver Licenses:*
Department of Motor Vehicles
Traffic Records
104 W. 6th Avenue, Rm 103
Denver, CO 80204
(303) 623-9463

*State Vehicle Titles/Registrations:*
Department of Motor Vehicles
Vehicle Records Section
140 W 6th Ave
Denver, CO 80204
(303) 623-9463

*State Archives:*
Colorado State Archives
Archives & Public Records Division
1313 Sherman Street, Room 1B-20
Denver, CO 80203
(303) 866-2358, (303) 866-2257 Fax
E-mail: archives@state.co.us

*State Historical Society:*
Colorado Historical Society
1300 Broadway
Denver, CO 80203-2137
(303) 866-2305

Council of Genealogical Societies
PO Box 24379
Denver, CO 80224-0379

Colorado Genealogical Society
PO Box 9218
Denver, CO 80209-0218

*Adoption Support Group:*
Adoptees Support Group
Christine Moran
420 N. Nevada
Colorado Springs, CO 80903
(719) 471-8522

*Adoption Researcher:*
Adoptees in Search/AIS
Beth Paddock-ISC
4631 Carter Trail
Boulder, CO 80301
(303) 530-7241, (303) 443-3425 Fax
E-mail: paddock2u@aol.com

State Adjutant General
6848 S. Revere Parkway
Englewood, CO 80112-6703
(303) 397-3173

VA Regional Office
155 Van Gordon Street
Denver, CO 80225
(800) 827-1000

## CONNECTICUT

Area codes for state: 203, 860
State government information number: (860) 566-2211
State prison locator: (860) 692-7480
State website: *www.state.ct.us*

Child Support Enforcement
PO Box 320650
Hartford, CT 06132
(800) 228-KIDS, (860) 566-4098
(860) 566-8949 Fax

*State Vital Statistics:*
Department of Public Health
Vital Records Section
410 Capitol Avenue
Hartford, CT 061134-0308
(860) 509-7897
*Divorce decrees are county records.

*State Driver Licenses:*
Department of Motor Vehicles
Copy Records Section
60 State Street, Room 305
Wethersfield, CT 06161
(860) 566-7740

*State Vehicle Titles/Registrations:*
Department of Motor Vehicles
Copy Record Unit
60 State St, Branch Operations
Wethersfield, CT 06161
(860) 566-3090

*State Archives:*
Connecticut State Library
Archives Division
231 Capitol Avenue
Hartford, CT 06106
(860) 566-3692
(860) 566-2133 Fax

State Historical Society
Connecticut Historical Commission
59 South Prospect Street
Hartford, CT 06106
(860) 566-3005

Connecticut Historical Society
1 Elizabeth Street at Asylum Avenue
Hartford, CT 06105
(860) 236-5621, (860) 236-2664 Fax

Conn. League of Historical Societies
2105 Chester Village West
Chester, CT 06412-1040

Connecticut Society of Genealogists
175 Maple Street
East Hartford, CT 06118
(860) 569-0002

*Adoption Support Group:*
Adoption Healing
Barbara Wille
2 Hadik Parkway #F2
S. Norwalk, CT 06854
(203) 866-6475

*Adoption Researcher:*
Ties That Bind
Jane Servadio
Box 3119
Milford, CT 06460
(203) 874-2023

State Adjutant General
360 Broad Street
Hartford, CT 06105-3795
(860) 524-4820, (860) 524-4989 Fax

VA Regional Office
450 Main Street
Hartford, CT 06103
(800) 827-1000

## DELAWARE

Area code for state: 302
State government information number: (800) 273-9500
State prison locator: (302) 739-5601
State website: *www.state.de.us*

Child Support Enforcement Office
PO Box 904
New Castle, DE 19720
(302) 577-4840, (302) 577-4873 Fax

*State Vital Statistics:*
Division of Public Health
Office of Vital Statistics
PO Box 637
Dover, DE 19903
(302) 739-4721
*Divorce decrees are county records.

*State Driver Licenses:*
Division of Motor Vehicles
Driver Services
PO Box 698
Dover, DE 19903
(302) 739-4343

*State Vehicle Titles/Registrations:*
Division of Motor Vehicles
ATTN: Correspondence Section
PO Box 698
Dover, DE 19903
(302) 739-3147

*State Archives:*
Department of Public Archives
Hall of Records
121 Duke of York Street
Dover, DE 19901
(302) 739-5318, (302) 739-2578 Fax

Historical Society of Delaware
5050 Market Street
Wilmington, DE 19801-3091
(302) 655-7161

Delaware Genealogical Society
505 Market Street Mall
Wilmington, DE 19801-3091

*Adoption Support Group/ Researcher:*
Finders Keepers, Inc.
Ginger Farrow
Box 748
Bear, DE 19701-0748
(302) 834-8888

State Adjutant General
1st Regiment Rd.
Wilmington, DE 19808-2191
(302) 326-7043
(302) 326-7196 Fax

VA Regional Office
1601 Kirkwood Highway
Wilmington, DE 19805
(800) 827-1000

## DISTRICT OF COLUMBIA

Area code for district: 202
DC government operator: (202) 727-1000
DC website: *www.washdc.org*

*District Vital Statistics:*
Department of Health
Vital Records Branch
613 "G" Street, NW, 9th Flr
Washington, DC 20001
(202) 727-9281
*birth and death records.

Superior Court House
500 Indiana Avenue, NW
Washington, DC 20001
Marriage: (202) 879-4850
Divorce: (202) 879-1410

*District Driver Licenses:*
Department of Motor Vehicles
Driver Records Division
301 "C" Street, NW, Rm 1157
Washington, DC 20001
(202) 727-6761

*District Vehicle Titles/Registrations:*
Department of Motor Vehicles
Vehicle Control Division
301 "C" Street, NW, Rm 1063
Washington, DC 20001
(202) 727-4768

*District Archives:*
Secretary of District of Columbia
Archives/Public Records Office
1300 Naylor Court, NW
Washington, DC 20001-4225
(202) 727-5052, (202) 727-6076 Fax

The Columbia Historical Society
1307 New Hampshire Avenue, NW
Washington, DC 20036
(202) 785-2068

U.S. Capitol Historical Society
200 Maryland Avenue, NE
Washington, DC 20002
(202) 543-8919

*Adoption Support Group:*
Adoptee Birthparent Support Network
3421 "M" Street, NW, #328
Washington, DC 20007
(202) 686-4611

VA Regional Office
1120 Vermont Ave, NW
Washington, DC 20421
(800) 827-1000

## FLORIDA

Area codes for state: 305, 321, 352, 407, 561, 727, 786, 813, 850, 863, 904, 941, 954
State government information number: (850) 488-1234
State prison locator: (850) 488-2533
State website: *www.state.fl.us*

*Child Support Enforcement Office:*
Child Support Enforcement
325 West Gaines Street
Tallahassee, FL 32399-3150
(800) 622-KIDS, (850) 922-9590
(850!) 488-4401 Fax

*State Vital Statistics:*
Florida Department of Health
Office of Vital Statistics
PO Box 210
Jacksonville, FL 32231
(904) 359-6900

*State Driver Licenses:*
Department of Public Safety
Division of Drivers Licenses
2900 Apalachee Pkwy, Rm B-239
Tallahassee, FL 32399
(850) 487-2369

*State Vehicle Titles/Registrations:*
Division of Motor Vehicles
Information Research Section
Niel Kirkman Building, Rm A-126
Tallahassee, FL 32399
(850) 488-5665

*State Archives:*
Library & Information Services Div.
Archives & Records
500 S. Bronough Street
Tallahassee, FL 32399-0250
(850) 487-2073, (850) 488-4894 Fax
E-mail: barm@mail.dos.state.fl.us

Florida Historical Society
University of South Florida Library
PO Box 290197
Tampa, FL 33687-0197
(813) 974-3815

Florida History Associates
R. A. Gray Building
500 South Bronough Street
Tallahassee, FL 32399-0250
(850) 488-1484

Florida Genealogical Society
PO Box 18624
Tampa, FL 33679-8624

Society for Genealogical Research
8461 54th Street, North
Pinellas Park, FL 33565
(813) 391-2914

Florida State Genealogical Society
PO Box 10249
Tallahassee, FL 32302-2249

*Adoption Support Group:*
Adoption Triangle
Pat Jakubek
1301 N.W. 2nd Avenue
Delray Beach, FL 33444
(407) 276-5737

*Adoption Researcher:*
Active Voices in Adoption
June Lewis
PO Box 24-9052
Coral Gables, FL 33124
(305) 667-0387, (305) 667-2601 Fax

State Adjutant General
PO Box 1008
St. Augustine, FL 32085-1008
(904) 823-0300, (904) 823-0125 Fax

VA Regional Office
144 First Avenue, S.
St. Petersburg, FL 33701
(800) 827-1000

## GEORGIA

Area codes for state: 404, 678, 706, 770, 912
State government information number: (404) 656-2000
State prison locator: (404) 656-4605
State website: *www.state.ga.us*

Child Support Enforcement Office
#2 Peachtree Street
15th Floor, Suite 100
Atlanta, GA 30303
(800) 227-7993, (404) 657-3851
(404) 657-3326 Fax

*State Vital Statistics:*
Georgia Dept. of Human Resources
Vital Records Unit, Rm 217-H
47 Trinity Ave SW
Atlanta, GA 30334-4750
(404) 656-4750
*Divorce decrees are county records.

*State Driver Licenses:*
Department of Motor Vehicles
Drivers License Section
MVR Unit, PO Box 1456
Atlanta, GA 30371
(404) 624-7487

*State Vehicle Titles/Registrations:*
Department of Revenue Research
270 Washington St, SW, Rm 105
Atlanta, GA 30334
(404) 656-4156

*State Archives:*
Archives and Records Bldg.
330 Capitol Avenue, SE
Atlanta, GA 30334
(404) 656-2393, (404) 657-8427 Fax

Georgia Historical Society
501 Whittaker Street
Savannah, GA 31499
(912) 651-2128

*Adoption Support Group:*
Adoptee Birthparent Connection
Susan Russell
4565 Pond Lane
Marrietta, GA 30062
(770) 642-9063

*Adoption Researcher:*
Adoption Beginnings
Georgi Tanis
Box 440121
Kennesaw, GA 30144
(404) 841-6677 Fax

State Adjutant General
PO Box 17965
Atlanta, GA 30316-0965
(404) 624-5006, (404) 624-6005 Fax

VA Regional Office
730 Peachtree St, NE
Atlanta, GA 30365
(800) 827-1000

## HAWAII

Area code for state: 808
State government information number: (808) 586-2211
State prison locator: (808) 587-1258
State website: *www.state.hi.us*

*State Child Support Enforcement Office:*
Hawaii Child Support Enforcement Agency
PO Box 2310
Honolulu, HI 96804
(800) 468-4644, (808) 587-3712
(808) 587-3673 Fax

*State Vital Statistics:*
Office of Health Status Monitoring
Vital Records Section
PO Box 3378
Honolulu, HI 96801
(808) 586-4535
*Hawaii does not release information to the public without a signed release from the person being sought, or immediate family can request records.

*State Driver Licenses:*
Traffic Violations Bureau
Abstract Section
1111 Alakea Street
Honolulu, HI 96813
(808) 538-5530
*Addresses are not available.

*State Vehicle Titles/Registrations:*
*Vehicle identifications, registrations, and title histories are not available to the public.

*State Archives:*
General Services Department
Archives Division
Iolani Palace Grounds
Kekaulouhi Building
Honolulu, HI 96813
(808) 586-0329, (808) 586-0330 Fax

Hawaiian Historical Society
560 Kawaiahao Street
Honolulu, HI 96813
(808) 537-6271

Sandwich Islands Geneal. Society
Hawaii State Library
478 South King Street
Honolulu, HI 96813

*Adoption Support Group:*
Triad Resources for Adoption
Martha W. Hurlbert
55 Niuiki Circle
Honolulu, HI 96821
(808) 377-2345

*Adoption Researcher:*
Claudia Clienke-ISC
Box 1120
Hilo, HI 96721-1120
(808) 965-7185

State Adjutant General
3949 Diamond Head Road
Honolulu, HI 96818-4495
(808) 753-4243

VA Regional Office
PO Box 50188
Honolulu, HI 96850-0188
(800) 827-1000

## IDAHO

Area code for state: 208
State government information number: (208) 334-2411
State prison locator: (208) 658-2000
State website: *www.state.id.us*

Child Support Enforcement Office
PO Box 83720
Boise, ID 83720-0036
(800) 356-9868
(208) 334-5710
(208) 334-0666 Fax

*State Vital Statistics:*
State Department of Health
Vital Statistics
PO Box 83720
Boise, ID 83720-0036
(208) 334-5988

*State Driver Licenses:*
Idaho Transportation Department
Drivers Services
PO Box 34
Boise, ID 83701
(208) 334-8736

*State Vehicle Titles/Registrations:*
Idaho Transportation Department
Titles/Dealers Operations Section
PO Box 7129
Boise, ID 83707
(208) 334-8663

*State Archives:*
Idaho State Historical Society
1109 Main Street, Suite 250
Boise, ID 83702
(208) 334-2120, (208) 334-4059 Fax

The Idaho State Historical Society
Genealogical Library
450 North Fourth Street
Boise, ID 83702-6027
(208) 334-3356, (208) 334-3198 Fax

The Idaho Genealogical Society
4620 Overland Road, #204
Boise, ID 83705-2867
(208) 384-0542

*Adoption Support Group:*
Adopted Child
Lois Melina
PO Box 9362
Moscow, ID 83843
(208) 882-1794, (208) 883-8035 Fax
E-mail: lmelina@moscow.com

Adoption Support Group
PO Box 1435
Ketchum. ID 83340

*Adoption Researcher:*
SearchLight
Jesse Lassandro
PO Box 5341
Coeur d'Alene, ID 83814
(208) 689-3255

State Adjutant General
4040 W. Guard Street
Boise, ID 83705-5004
(208) 389-5242

VA Regional Office
805 W. Franklin Street
Boise, ID 83702
(800) 827-1000

## ILLINOIS

Area codes for state: 217, 224, 309, 312, 618, 630, 708, 773, 815, 847
State government information number: (217) 782-2000
State prison locator: (217) 522-2666, Ext 6489
State website: *www.state.il.us*

Child Support Enforcement Office
PO Box 19405
Springfield, IL 62794
(800) 723-KIDS
(800) 447-4278
(217) 524-1218 Fax

*State Vital Statistics:*
Illinois Department of Public Health
Division of Vital Records
605 West Jefferson Street
Springfield, IL 62702-5097
(217) 782-6554
*Divorce decrees are county records.

*State Driver Licenses:*
Driver Analysis Section
Drivers Services Department
2701 S. Kirksen Parkway
Springfield, IL 62723
(217) 782-2720

*State Vehicle Titles/Registrations:*
Vehicle Services Department
Record Inquiry
408 Howlett Building
Springfield, IL 62756
(217) 782-6992

*State Archives:*
Illinois State Archives
Margaret Cross Norton Building
Capitol Complex
Springfield, IL 62756
(217) 782-4682
(217) 524-3930 Fax

Illinois Genealogical Society
Old State Capitol
Springfield, IL 62701
(217) 785-7938

Illnois State Historical Society
1 Old State Capitol Plaza
Springfield, IL 62701
(217) 524-6045

Illiniois Historic Preservation Agency
Old State Capitol
1 Old State Capitol Plaza
Springfield, IL 62701
(217) 524-6045

Illinois State Genealogical Society
PO Box 10195
Springfield, IL 62791-0195
(217) 789-1968

*Adoption Support Group:*
Adoption Triangle
Lydia Granda
512 Oneida Street
Joliet, IL 60435
(815) 722-4999

*Adoption Researcher:*
Beth Duensing
PO Box 384
Park Forest, IL 60466
(708) 481-8916
E-mail: bethd@nitco.com

Truth Seekers in Adoption
PO Box 366
Prospect Heights, IL 60070

State Adjutant General
1301 N. MacArthur Blvd.
Springfield, IL 62702-2399
(217) 761-3540

VA Regional Office
536 S. Clark Street
Chicago, IL 60605-1523

## INDIANA

Area codes for state: 219, 317, 765, 812
State government information number: (317) 232-1000
State prison locator: (317) 232-5715
State website: *www.state.in.us*

*Child Support Enforcement Office:*
Family & Social Services Admin.
Division of Family and Child
Child Support Section
402 W. Washington St, Rm W-461
Indianapolis, IN 46201
(800) 622-4932, (317) 233-4454
(317) 233-4925 Fax

*State Vital Statistics:*
State Department of Health
Vital Records Section
2 N. Meridian Street
Indianapolis, IN 46204
(317) 233-2700
*Divorce decrees are county records.

*State Driver Licenses:*
Bureau of Motor Vehicles
Driver Records, Rm N-405
Indiana Government Center North
Indianapolis, IN 46204
(317) 232-2894

*State Vehicle Titles/Registrations:*
Bureau of Motor Vehicles
Vehicle Records
100 N. Senate Ave, Rm N-405
Indianapolis, IN 46204

*State Archives:*
Public Records Commission
Archive Division
402 W. Washington St, Rm W-472
Indianapolis, IN 46204
(317) 232-3660
(317) 233-3154 Fax

Indiana Historical Society
State Library & Historical Bldg.
315 West Ohio Street
PO Box 88255
Indianapolis, IN 46202
(317) 233-3157

Indiana Genealogical Society
PO Box 10507
Fort Wayne, IN 46852-0507

*Adoption Support Group:*
Anonymous By Adoption
Tina Miller-Irmscher
PO Box 12034
Ft. Wayne, IN 46862-2034
(219) 744-1518

*Adoption Researcher:*
Catholic Charities
Deb Schmidt
315 E. Washington Blvd.
Ft. Wayne, IN 46802
(219) 439-0242, (219) 430-0250 Fax
E-mail: UBRHOOA@prodigy.com

State Adjutant General
2002 S. Holt Road
Indianapolis, IN 46241-4839
(317) 247-3219

VA Regional Office
575 N. Pennsylvania Street
Indianapolis, IN 46204
(800) 827-1000

## IOWA

Area codes for state: 319, 515, 712
State government information number: (515) 281-5011
State prison locator: (515) 281-4816 or (515) 242-5701
State website: *www.state.ia.us*

Child Support Enforcement Office
15th Floor SW, Hoover Building
Des Moines, IA 50319
(515) 281-5580
(515) 281-8854 Fax

*State Vital Statistics:*
Iowa Department of Public Health
Vital Records Section
Lucas Office Building
321 E. 12th St, 1st Floor
Des Moines, IA 50319-0075
(515) 281-4944
*Divorce decrees are county records.

*State Driver Licenses:*
Department of Transportation
Driver Service Records Section
PO Box 9204
Des Moines, IA 50306-9204
(515) 244-9124, (515) 237-3152 Fax

*State Vehicle Titles/Registrations:*
Department of Transportation
Office of Vehicle Registration
PO Box 9204
Des Moines, IA 50306-9204
(515) 237-3110, (515) 237-3181 Fax

State Archives of Iowa
600 E. Locust, Capitol Complex
Des Moines, IA 50319
(515) 281-5111, (515) 282-0502 Fax

Iowa Genealogical Society
6000 Douglas
PO Box 7735
Des Moines, IA 50322

*Adoption Support Group:*
Concerned United Birthparents
2000 Walker Street
Des Moines, IA 50317
(515) 263-9558, (515) 263-9541 Fax

*Adoption Researcher:*
Origins, Inc.
Jim McDonald
4300 Ashby Avenue
Des Moines, IA 50310-3540
(515) 277-7700, (515) 277-9811 Fax

*Adoption Registry:*
Iowa Reunion Registry
Doris Smith
PO Box 8
Blairsburg, IA 50034

State Adjutant General
7700 N.W. Beaver Drive
Johnston, IA 50131-1902
(515) 252-4360

VA Regional Office
210 Walnut Street
Des Mones, IA 50309
(800) 827-1000

## KANSAS

Area codes for state: 316, 785, 913
State government information number: (913) 296-0111
State prison locator: (785) 296-7220
State website: *www.state.ks.us*

Child Support Enforcement Office
PO Box 497
Topeka, KS 66601
(785) 296-3237, (785) 296-5206 Fax

*State Vital Statistics:*
Kansas State Dept of Health
and Environment
Office of Vital Statistics
900 SW Jackson Street, Suite 151
Topeka, KS 66612
(785) 296-1400

*State Driver Licenses:*
Department of Revenue
Driver Control Bureau
PO Box 12021
Topeka, KS 66612
(785) 296-3671

*State Vehicle Titles/Registrations:*
Division of Vehicles
Title and Registration Bureau
915 Harrison
Topeka, KS 66616
(785) 296-3621

*State Archives:*
Historical Society, Archives Dept.
120 W. 10th Street
Topeka, KS 66612
(785) 296-4792, (785) 296-1005 Fax

Kansas State Historical Society
Reference Services
120 W. 10th Street
Topeka, KS 66612
(785) 296-4776

Council of Genealogical Societies
PO Box 3858
Topeka, KS 66604-6858
(785) 774-4411

Kansas Genealogical Society
700 Avenue G at Vine Street
PO Box 103
Dodge City, KS 67801-0103
(316) 225-1951

*Adoption Support Group:*
Wichita Adult Adoptees
Rochelle Harris
4551 S. Osage Street
Wichita, KS 67217
(316) 522-8772

*Adoption Researcher:*
TRIAD Investigations
Joanne Brooks
PO Box 25705
Overland Park, KS 66225
(913) 491-8266

State Adjutant General
2800 S.W. Topeka Blvd
Topeka, KS 66611-1287
(785) 274-1061

VA Regional Office
5500 E. Kellogg
Wichita, KS 67211
(800) 827-1000

## KENTUCKY

Area codes for state: 270, 502, 606, 859
State government information number: (502) 564-3130
State prison locator: (502) 564-2433
State website: *www.state.ky.us*

*Child Support Enforcement Office:*
Cabinet for Families and Children
Department for Social Insurance
Div. of Child Support Enforcement
PO Box 2150
Frankfort, KY 40602-2150
(800) 248-1163, (502) 564-2285
(502) 564-5988 Fax

*State Vital Statistics:*
Cabinet for Health Services
Office of Vital Statistics
275 East Main Street
Frankfort, KY 40621
(502) 564-4212

*State Driver Licenses:*
Division of Drivers Licensing
MCRS-State Office Building
501 High Street, 2nd Floor
Frankfort, KY 40622
(502) 564-4711

*State Vehicle Titles/Registrations:*
Department of Motor Vehicles
Division of Motor Vehicle Licensing
State Office Building, 3rd Floor
Frankfort, KY 40622
(502) 564-2737, (502) 564-4076

*State Archives:*
Dept. of Libraries & Archives
PO Box 537
300 Coffee Tree Road
Frankfort, KY 40602-0537
(502) 564-8300, (502) 564-5773 Fax

Historical Confed. of Kentucky
PO Box H
Frankfort, KY 40602-2108
(502) 564-3016, (502) 564-4701 Fax

Kentucky Historical Society
300 Broadway, Old Capitol Annex
Frankfort, KY 40601
PO Box H
Frankfort, KY 40602-2108

*Adoption Support Group:*
Concerned United Birthparents
Sherry Szewczykowski
PO Box 22795
Louisville, KY 40252
(502) 423-1438

*Adoption Registry:*
Adoption Reunion Registry
Linda Cecil
PO Box 1218
Nicholsville, KY 40356
(800) 755-7954, (606) 885-1778 Fax
E-mail: lcecil@aol.com

State Adjutant General
Boone National Guard Center
Frankfort, KY 40601-6168
(502) 564-8446

VA Regional Office
545 S. Third Street
Louisville, KY 40202
(800) 827-1000

## LOUISIANA

Area code for state: 225, 318, 337, 504
State government information number: (225) 342-6600, (800) 256-7777
State prison locator: (225) 297-2000
State website: *www.state.la.us*

Child Support Enforcement Office
618 Main Street
Baton Rouge, LA 70802
(800) 256-4650
(225) 342-4780

*State Vital Statistics:*
Department of Public Health
Vital Records Registry
PO Box 60630
New Orleans, LA 70160
(504) 568-5163
*Divorce/marriage are county records.

*State Driver Licenses & Vehicle Titles/Registrations:*
Department of Public Safety & Corrections
Office of Motor Vehicles
109 W. Foster Drive
Baton Rouge, LA 70806
(225) 925-6009 (driver licenses/records)
(225) 925-6146 (titles/registrations)
*Same address for driver records and titles.

*State Archives:*
Secretary of State
Archives & Records Division
3851 Essen Lane
Baton Rouge, LA 70809-2137
(225) 922-1184
(225) 922-0433 Fax

Louisiana Historical Society
PO Box 789
Kinder, LA 70648-0789

LA Genealogical & Historical Society
PO Box 3454
Baton Rouge, LA 70821

*Adoption Support Group:*
Adoptees & Birthparents Committee
Mary D. Langhetee
Box 9442
Metairie, LA 70005
(504) 888-7963, (504) 837-4768 Fax

Adoption Triad Network
Johnnie Kocurek
120 Thibodeaux Dr.
Lafayette, LA 70503
(318) 984-3682

*Adoption Researcher:*
Mary Ellen Davros
511 Blue Bell St.
Port Allen, LA 70605
(504) 344-8373
(504) 336-4750 Fax

State Adjutant General
Hdq Bldg Jackson Barracks
New Orleans, LA 70146-0330
(504) 278-6311

VA Regional Office
PO Box 94095, Capital Stn.
Baton Rouge, LA 70804-9095
(800) 827-1000

## MAINE

Area code for state: 207
State government information number: (207) 582-9500
State prison locator: (207) 354-2535
State website: *www.state.me.us*

*Child Support Enforcement Office:*
Division of Human Services
Support Enforcement and Recovery
219 Capitol Street
State House Station 11
Augusta, ME 04330
(800) 371-3101, (207) 624-8320
(207) 624-8074 Fax

*State Vital Statistics:*
Maine Dept. of Human Services
Vital Statistics
State House Station 11
Augusta, ME 04333-0011
(207) 287-3184

*State Driver Licenses:*
Bureau of Motor Vehicles
Driver License and Control
State House Station 29
Augusta, ME 04333
(207) 287-2576

*State Vehicle Titles/Registrations:*
Department of Motor Vehicles
Registration Section
State House Station 29
Augusta, ME 04333
(207) 287-3556

State Archives
84 State House Station
Augusta, ME 04333-0084
(207) 287-5795, (207) 287-5739 Fax

Maine Historical Society
485 Congress Street
Portland, ME 04101
(207) 774-1822

Maine Genealogical Society
PO Box 221
Farmington, ME 04938-0221

*Adoption Support Group:*
M. Bicknell Adoption Resource Cntr.
Brenda Peluso
PO Box 2793
South Portland, ME 04116
(207) 773-3378
E-mail: brenluso@aol.com

*Adoption Researcher:*
The Adoption Counsel
Sheridan D. Robbins
34 Winn Road
Falmouth, ME 04105-1128
(207) 797-0983

State Adjutant General
Camp Keyes
Augusta, ME 04333-0033
(207) 626-4317

VA Regional Office
Route 17 East
Togus, ME 04330
(800) 827-1000

## MARYLAND

Area codes for state: 240, 301, 410, 443
State government information number: None available.
State prison locator: (410) 764-4100
State website: *www.state.md.us*

Child Support Enforcement Office
Department of Human Resources
311 W. Saratoga St, 3rd Floor
Baltimore, MD 21201
(800) 638-3912, (410) 333-6500
(410) 333-8992 Fax

*State Vital Statistics:*
Department of Health
Division of Vital Records
6550 Reistertown Road
Baltimore, MD 21215
(410) 764-3038, (800) 832-3277

*State Driver Licenses:*
Division of Motor Vehicles
Motor Vehicle Administration
6601 Rickie Hwy, NE
Glen Burnie, MD 21062
(410) 787-7705

*State Vehicle Titles/Registrations:*
Department of Motor Vehicles
Vehicle Registration Division
6601 Rickie Hwy, NE, Rm 206
Glen Burnie, MD 21062
(410) 768-7250

*State Archives:*
Maryland State Archives
350 Rowe Blvd.
Annapolis, MD 21401
(410) 260-6400, (800) 235-4045
(410) 974-3895 Fax
E-mail:
archives@mdarchives.state.md.us
Website: *www.mdsa.net*

Maryland Historical Society
201 West Monument Street
Baltimore, MD 21201
(410) 685-3750, Ext 360

Maryland Genealogical Society
201 West Monument Street
Baltimore, MD 21201
(410) 685-3750, Ext 360

*Adoption Support Group:*
Adoptee/Birthparent Support Net.
Anne Bowman
3002 Lake Ave.
Cheverly, MD 20785
(301) 773-1286

*Adoption Researcher:*
Robyn Quinter
3307 Gold Mine Road
Brookeville, MD 20833
(301) 924-2471

*Adoption Registry:*
Mutual Consent Voluntary
Adoption Registry
Sharon Hackett
311 W. Saratoga St
Baltimore, MD 21201
(410) 767-7372, (410) 333-0392 Fax

State Adjutant General
5th Regiment Armory
Baltimore, MD 21201-2288
(410) 576-6011

VA Regional Office
Federal Bldg, Rm 110
31 Hopkins Plaza
Baltimore, MD 21201
(800) 827-1000

## MASSACHUSETTS

Area codes for state: 413, 508, 617, 781, 978
State government information number: (617) 727-7030
State prison locator: (617) 727-3300
State website: *www.state.ma.us*

*Child Support Enforcement Office:*
Department of Revenue
Child Support Enforcement Office
51 Sleeper Street
Boston, MA 02210
(800) 332-2733, (617) 626-4000
(617) 727-1320 Fax

*State Vital Statistics:*
Registry Vital Records/Statistics
470 Atlantic Ave, 2nd Floor
Boston, MA 02111
(617) 753-8600
*Divorce decrees are county records.

*Vehicle Titles/Registrations, Driver Licenses:*
Registry of Motor Vehicles
Customer Assistance
Mail Listing Dept.
630 Washington Street
Boston, MA 02111-1615
(617) 351-4500

*State Archives:*
Massachusetts Archives
220 Morrissey Blvd
Boston, MA 02125-3384
(617) 727-2816
(617) 288-8429 Fax

Massachusetts Historical Society
1154 Boylston Street
Boston, MA 02215
(617) 536-1608

Massachusetts Genealogical Council
PO Box 5393
Cochituate, MA 01778

Massachusetts Society of Genealogists
PO Box 215
Ashland, MA 01721-0215

*Adoption Support Group:*
Adoption Healing
Carolyn Canfield
87 Chestnut Street
E. Falmouth, MA 02536
(508) 457-7181, (508) 457-4875 Fax

TRY - Resource Referral Center
Ann Patnaude-Henry
PO Box 989
Northampton, MA 01061-0989
(413) 584-6599, (413) 568-3663 Fax

*Adoption Researcher:*
Adoption Triad
10 W. Hollow Lane
Webster, MA 01570
(508) 949-1919

Adoption Resource Center
PO Box 383246
Cambridge, MA 02238-3246

State Adjutant General
50 Maple Street
Milford, MA 01757-3604
(508) 233-6621

VA Regional Office
JFK Federal Bldg, Govt. Ctr
Boston, MA 02203
(800) 827-1000

## MICHIGAN

Area codes for state: 231, 248, 313, 517, 616, 734, 810, 906
State government information number: (517) 373-1837
State prison locator: (517) 335-1426
State website: *www.state.mi.us*

Child Support Enforcement Office
PO Box 30478
Lansing, MI 48909-7978
(517) 373-7570
(517) 373-4980 Fax

*State Vital Statistics:*
Michigan Department of Health
Vital Records & Health Statistics
3423 N. Martin Luther King Blvd.
Lansing, MI 48909
(517) 335-8666

*State Driver Licenses/ Vehicle Titles/Registrations:*
Department of State Police
Commercial Look-up Unit
7064 Crowner Drive
Lansing, MI 48918
(517) 322-1624
*Same office for driving records and title/registration.

*State Archives:*
Mich. Library & Historical Cntr.
Archives Division
717 W. Allegan Street
Lansing, MI 48918-1837
(517) 373-1408
(517) 241-1658 Fax

Michigan Historical Commission
505 State Office Building
Lansing, MI 48913

Historical Society of Michigan
2117 Washtenaw Avenue
Ann Arbor, MI 48104
(313) 769-1828

Michigan Genealogical Council
PO Box 80953
Lansing, MI 48908-0953

*Adoption Support Group:*
Adoption Identity Movement
Peg Richer
PO Box 9265
Grand Rapids, MI 49509
(616) 531-1380, (616) 532-5589 Fax

*Adoption Researcher:*
Christine Buehrer-ISC
1270 Grosvenor Hwy.
Palmyra, MI 49268
(517) 486-3444

State Adjutant General
2500 S. Washington Avenue
Lansing, MI 48913-5101
(517) 483-5514

VA Regional Office
477 Michigan Avenue
Detroit, MI 48226
(800) 827-1000

## MINNESOTA

Area codes for state: 218, 320, 507, 612, 651
State government information number: (612) 296-6013
State prison locator: (612) 642-0322
State website: *www.state.mn.us*

Child Support Enforcement Office
449 Lafayette Road
St. Paul, MN 55155-3846
(651) 296-2499
(651) 297-4450 Fax

*State Vital Statistics:*
Minnesota Department of Health
Section of Vital Records
717 Delaware Street, SE
Minneapolis, MN 55440-9441
(612) 676-5120
*Divorce and marriage records are at county level.

*State Vehicle Titles/Registrations:*
Driver and Vehicle Services
Records Department
395 John Ireland Blvd, Rm 214
St. Paul, MN 55155
(651) 296-6911

*State Archives:*
Minnesota Historical Society
Rsearch Center
345 Kellogg Blvd, W.
St. Paul, MN 55102-1906
(651) 296-6126
(651) 297-3343 Fax

Minnesota Genealogical Society
1650 Carroll Avenue
St. Paul, MN 55104
PO Box 16069 *(mail)*
St. Paul, MN 55116-0069
(651) 645-3671

*Adoption Support Group:*
Concerned United Birthparents
Sandra Sperrazza
6429 Mendelssohn Lane
Edina, MN 55343
(612) 938-5866

*Adoption Researcher:*
Liberal Education
for Adoptive Families
Cheryl Rock
23247 Lofton Court, North
N. Scandia, MN 55073
(612) 436-2215

*Adoption Registry:*
Minnesota Reunion Registry
Patty O'Gorman
23247 Lofton Court, North
N. Scandia, MN 55073
(612) 433-5211

CUB
6429 Mendelssohn Ln.
Edina, MN 55343

State Adjutant General
20 W. 12th Street
St. Paul, MN 55073-2098
(651) 282-4040

VA Regional Office
1 Federal Drive
St. Paul, MN 55111
(800) 827-1000

## MISSISSIPPI

Area code for state: 228, 601, 662
State government information number: (601) 359-1000
State prison locator: (601) 745-6611
State website: *www.state.ms.us*

Div. of Child Support Enforcement
PO Box 352
750 North State Street
Jackson, MS 39205
(800) 948-4010, (601) 354-0341
(601) 359-4415 Fax
E-mail: rharris@mdhs.state.ms.us

*State Vital Statistics:*
State Department of Health
Public Health Statistics
PO Box 1700
Jackson, MS 39215-1700
(601) 576-7960, (601) 576-7517 Fax
E-mail: info@msdh.state.ms.us

*State Driver Licenses:*
Department of Public Safety
Driver Records
PO Box 958
Jackson, MS 39205
(601) 987-1212

*State Vehicle Titles/Registrations:*
Mississippi State Tax Commission
Registration Department
PO Box 1140
Jackson, MS 39215-1140
(601) 359-1248

*State Archives:*
Archives & History Department
Capers Building
100 South State Street
PO Box 571
Jackson, MS 39205-0571
(601) 359-6876
(601) 359-6964 Fax

MS Historical & Genealogical Assn.
618 Avalon Road
Jackson, MS 39206
(601) 362-3079

Mississippi Historical Society
PO Box 571
Jackson, MS 39205-0571
(601) 359-6850

Mississippi Genealogical Society
PO Box 5301
Jackson, MS 39296-5301

*Adoption Support Group:*
Adoption Information Network
PO Box 4154
Meridian, MS 39304

Mississippi Adoption Network
30 N. Hill Pkway #B-4
Jackson, MS 39206-5591

State Adjutant General
PO Box 5027
Jackson, MS 39296-5027
(601) 973-6324

VA Regional Office
206 Pearl Street
Jackson, MS 39201
(800) 827-1000

## MISSOURI

Area codes for state: 314, 417, 573, 636, 660, 816
State government information number: (573) 751-2000
State prison locator: (573) 751-2389
State website: *www.state.mo.us*

*Child Support Enforcement Office:*
Missouri Dept. of Social Services
Div. of Child Support Enforcement
227 Metro Drive
PO Box 1468
Jefferson City, MO 65102-1468
(800) 859-7999, (573) 751-4224
(573) 751-1257 Fax
E-mail: askcse@mail.state.mo.us

*State Vital Statistics:*
Missouri Department of Health
Bureau of Vital Records
PO Box 570
Jefferson City, MO 65102
(573) 751-6400
*Divorce/marriage are county records.

*State Driver Licenses:*
Department of Revenue
Driver License Bureau
PO Box 100
Jefferson City, MO 65105-0100
(573) 751-4600

*State Vehicle Titles/Registrations:*
Department of Motor Vehicles
Motor Vehicle Bureau
PO Box 100
Jefferson City, MO 65105
(573) 751-4509

*State Archives:*
Missouri State Archives
State Information Center
PO Box 1747
Jefferson City, MO 65102-0778
(573) 751-3280, (573) 526-7333 Fax
E-mail: archref@sosmail.state.mo.us

Missouri Historical Society
Research Library & Archives
Jefferson Memorial Building
225 S. Skinker
St. Louis, MO 63112-1099
(314) 746-4500

Missouri State Genealogical Assn.
PO Box 833
Columbia, MO 65205-0833

*Adoption Support Group:*
Kansas City Adult Adoptees
Sandy Hassler
PO Box 11828
Kansas City, MO 64138
(816) 229-4075
E-mail: ulqq10a@prodigy.com

*Adoption Researcher:*
Adoptee Searches, Inc.
Virginia Long
PO Box 803
Chesterfield, MO 63006
(800) 434-0020
(314) 561-5005 Fax

*Adoption Registry:*
Donors Offspring
Candace Turner
PO Box 37
Sarcoxie, MO 64862
(417) 434-0020
(417) 673-1906 Fax

State Adjutant General
2302 Militia Drive
Jefferson City, MO 65101
(573) 638-9500

VA Regional Office
400 South 18th Street
St. Louis, MO 63103
(800) 827-1000

## MONTANA

Area code for state: 406
State government information number: (406) 444-2511
State prison locator: (406) 444-9521, (800) 456-3076
State website: *www.state.mt.us*

*State Child Support Enforcement Office:*
Dept. of Health & Human Services
Child Support Enforcement Division
PO Box 202943
Helena, MT 59620-2943
(800) 346-KIDS, (406) 442-7243
(406) 444-1370 Fax

*State Vital Statistics:*
Dept. of Health & Human Services
Vital Statistics Bureau
PO Box 4210
Helena, MT 56604-4210
(406) 444-4228
*Divorce/marriage are county records.

*State Driver Licenses:*
Motor Vehicle Division
Drivers Services
PO Box 201419
Helena, MT 59620
(406) 444-4590

*State Vehicle Titles and Registrations:*
Department of Justice
Title & Registration Bureau
925 Main Street
Deer Lodge, MT 59722
(406) 846-1423

*State Archives:*
Historical Society
Archives Division
225 N. Roberts Street
Helena, MT 59620
(406) 444-2694
(406) 444-2696 Fax

Montana Historical Society
Memorial Building
225 N. Roberts Street
Helena, MT 59620
(406) 444-2681

Montana State Genealogical Society
PO Box 555
Chester, MT 59522

*Adoption Support Group:*
Missoula Adoption Reunion Registry
Karen Virts
4104 Barbara Lane
Missoula, MT 59803
(406) 251-4158

*Adoption Researcher:*
Family Answers
Rosemary Furnell
214 12th Avenue, S.
Shelby, MT 59474
(406) 434-2548
E-mail: rfurnell@aol.com

Montana Post-Adoption Center
PO Box 634
Helena, MT 59624

State Adjutant General
PO Box 4789
Helena, MT 59604-4788
(406) 444-6925

VA Regional Office
PO Box 5715
Helena, MT 59604
(800) 827-1000

## NEBRASKA

Area codes for state: 308, 402
State government information number: (402) 471-2311
State prison locator: (402) 471-2654
State website: *www.state.ne.us*

*State Child Support Enforcement Office:*
Nebraska Dept of Health
& Human Services
PO Box 95026
Lincoln, NE 68509-5044
(402) 471-3121

*State Vital Statistics:*
Nebraska Dept of Health
& Human Services
Vital Records
PO Box 95065
Lincoln, NE 68509-5065
(402) 471-2871

*State Driver Licenses:*
Department of Motor Vehicles
Driver Records
PO Box 94789
Lincoln, NE 68509
(402) 471-4343

*State Vehicle Titles/Registrations:*
Department of Motor Vehicles
Titles & Registration Section
State Office Building
301 Centennial Mall, South
Lincoln, NE 68509
(402) 471-3918, (402) 471-8288 Fax

*State Archives:*
Nebraska State Historical Society
PO Box 82554
Lincoln, NE 68501-2554
(402) 471-3270, (402) 471-3100 Fax

Nebraska State Historical Society Room
Chadron State College
Chadron State Library
Chadron, NE 69337

*Adoption Support Group:*
Adoption Triad Midwest-Omaha
Marge Brower, PO Box 489
Fullerton, NE 68638
(308) 536-2633

*Adoption Researcher:*
Alice Beyke-ISC
1850 S. Baltimore
Hastings, NE 68901
(402) 462-6349

State Adjutant General
1300 Military Road
Lincoln, NE 68508-1090
(402) 471-7115

VA Regional Office
5631 S. 48th Street
Lincoln, NE 68516
(800) 827-1000

## NEVADA

Area code for state: 702, 775
State government information number: (775) 687-5000
State prison locator: (775) 887-3285
State website: *www.state.nv.us*

Nevada Child Support Enforcement
711 E. 5th Street
Carson City, NV 89710
(800) 992-0900
(775) 684-4400
(775) 684-4455 Fax

*State Vital Statistics:*
Department of Health
Office of Vital Statistics
505 East King Street
Carson City, NV 89710
(775) 687-4480

*Driver Licenses, Vehicle Titles and Registrations:*
Dept of Motor Vehicles & Public Safety
Records Section
555 Wright Way
Carson City, NV 89711
(775) 687-5505

*State Archives:*
Nevada State Library & Archives
Capitol Complex
100 N. Stewart Street
Carson City, NV 89701-4285
(775) 684-3310, (800) 922-2880

Nevada Historical Society
1650 North Virginia St
Reno, NV 89515
(775) 688-1190

Nevada State Genealogical Society
PO Box 20666
Reno, NV 89515

*Adoption Support Group:*
Adoptees Search Connection
Michael Sarkis
9713 Quail Springs Court
Las Vegas, NV 89117
(702) 363-2061

*Adoption Researcher:*
Truth of Adoption Searches & Support
1810 N. Decatur Blvd #204
Las Vegas, NV 89109
(702) 631-7101

State Adjutant General
2525 South Carson Street
Carson City, NV 89701-5502
(775) 887-7258

VA Regional Office
1201 Terminal Way, Rm 108
Reno, NV 89520
(800) 827-1000

## NEW HAMPSHIRE

Area code for state: 603
State government information number: (603) 271-1110
State prison locator: (603) 271-1823
State website: *www.state.nh.us*

*Child Support Enforcement Office:*
NH Division of Human Services
6 Hazen Drive
Concord, NH 03301-6505
(800) 852-3345, (603) 271-4426
(603) 271-4787 Fax

*State Vital Statistics:*
Bureau of Vital Records
Health and Welfare Building
6 Hazen Drive
Concord, NH 03301
(603) 271-4654

*State Driver Licenses:*
Department of Motor Vehicles
Driving Records
10 Hazen Drive
Concord, NH 03305-0002
(603) 271-2484

*State Vehicle Titles/Registrations:*
Department of Public Safety
Bureau of Title Registration
10 Hazen Drive
Concord, NH 03305
(603) 271-3111

*State Archives:*
Division of Records Management & Archives
71 S. Fruit Street
Concord, NH 03301
(603) 271-2236, (603) 271-2272 Fax

Assn of NH Historical Societies
11 Ironwood Lane
Atkinson, NH 03811-2706

NH Historical Society
30 Park Street
Concord, NH 03301
(603) 432-8137

NH Society of Genealogists
PO Box 633
Exeter, NH 03833-0633
(603) 432-8137

*Adoption Support Group:*
Adoption Bonding Circle
Karin Weigel
67 Ann Avenue
Charlestown, NH 03603-9630
(603) 826-4806

*Adoption Researcher:*
Circle of Hope
Karen Amos
PO Box 127
Somersworth, NH 03878
(603) 692-5917
E-mail: sbmm87a@prodigy.com

State Adjutant General
#1 Airport Road
Concord, NH 03301-5353
(603) 225-1200, (603) 225-1257

VA Regional Office
275 Chestnut Street
Manchester, NH 03101
(800) 827-1000

## NEW JERSEY

Area codes for state: 201, 609, 732, 856, 908, 973
State government information number: (609) 292-2121
State prison locator: (609) 292-0328
State website: *www.state.nj.us*

*Child Support Enforcement Office:*
New Jersey Dept of Human Services
Child Support & Paternity Program
CN-716
Trenton, NJ 08625
(800) 621-KIDS, (609) 588-2361
(609) 588-2354 Fax

*State Vital Statistics:*
State Department of Health
Vital Statistics
PO Box 370
Trenton, NJ 08625-0370
(609) 292-4087

*State Driver Licenses:*
Motor Vehicle Services
Drivers Abstract Section
CN-142
Trenton, NJ 08666
(609) 633-8255

*State Vehicle Titles/Registrations:*
Motor Vehicles Services
Certified Information Unit
PO Box 160
Trenton, NJ 08666
(609) 588-2424

*State Archives:*
New Jersey State Archives
PO Box 307
Trenton, NJ 08625-0307
(609) 292-6260, (609) 396-2454 Fax

New Jersey Historical Commission
20 West State Street, 4th Floor
PO Box 305
Trenton, NJ 08625-0305
(609) 292-6062, (609) 633-8168 Fax

Genealogical Society of New Jersey
PO Box 1291
New Brunswick, NJ 08903
(201) 356-6920

Library of NJ Historical Society
Genealogy Club
230 Broadway
Newark, NJ 07104
(201) 483-3939

*Adoption Support Group:*
Adoption Support Network
Janis Duncan, MSW
505 W. Hamilton Ave, #207
Linwood, NJ 08221
(609) 653-4242

*Adoption Researcher:*
NJ Services of the Missing
Nancy Heller
PO Box 26
Gibbsboro, NJ 08026
(609) 783-3101

State Adjutant General
Eggert Crossing Road, CN 340
Trenton, NJ 08625-0340
(609) 562-0652

VA Regional Office
20 Washington Place
Newark, NJ 07102
(800) 827-1000

## NEW MEXICO

Area code for state: 505
State government information number: (505) 827-9632
State prison locator: (505) 827-8710
State website: *www.state.nm.us*

Child Support Enforcement Office
PO Box 25110
Santa Fe, NM 87504
(800) 288-7207, (505) 476-7040
(505) 827-7285 Fax

*State Vital Statistics:*
Health Services Division
PO Box 26110
Santa Fe, NM 87502
(505) 827-2338, (505) 827-1751 Fax
*Divorce/marriage are county records.

*State Driver Licenses:*
Department of Motor Vehicles
Driver Services Bureau
PO Box 1028
Santa Fe, NM 87504
(505) 827-2241

*State Vehicle Titles/Registrations:*
Department of Motor Vehicles
Vehicle Service Bureau
PO Box 1028
Santa Fe, NM 87504
(505) 827-2220

*State Archives:*
State Records Center & Archives
1205 Camino Carlos Rey
Santa Fe, NM 87505
(505) 476-7900, (505) 476-7901 Fax
E-mail: asd@rain.state.nm.us

Historical Society of New Mexico
PO Box 1912
Santa Fe, NM 87504-1912

New Mexico Genealogical Society
PO Box 8283
Albuquerque, NM 87198-8283
(505) 256-3217

*Adoption Support Group:*
Operation Identity
Sally File
13101 Blackstone, NE
Albuquerque, NM 87111
(502) 293-3144

*Adoption Research:*
Concerned United Birthparents
Elizabeth Avens
358 Joya Loop
Los Alamos, NM 87544

State Adjutant General
47 Bataan Road
Santa Fe, NM 87505-4695
(505) 474-1255

VA Regional Office
500 Gold Avenue, SW
Albuquerque, NM 87102
(800) 827-1000

## NEW YORK

Area codes for state: 212, 315, 347, 516, 518, 607, 631, 646, 716, 718, 914, 917
State government information number: (518) 474-2121
State prison locator: (518) 457-0034
State website: *www.state.ny.us*

Office of Child Support Enforcement
40 N. Pearl Street
Albany, NY 12243
(800) 343-8859, (518) 474-9081
* or contact Dept. of DDS

*State Vital Statistics (but not NYC):*
State Department of Health
Vital Records Section
Empire State Plaza
Corning Tower Building
Albany, NY 12237-0023
(518) 474-3077

NYC Dept. of Health
Vital Records
125 Worth Street
New York, NY 10013
(212) 619-4530

*State Driver Licenses:*
Department of Motor Vehicles
6 Empire State Plaza
Albany, NY 12228
(518) 474-2381, (800) DIAL-DMV

*State Vehicle Titles/Registrations:*
Div. of Data Preparation & Control
Empire State Plaza
Swan State Building, Core 3
Albany, NY 12228
(518) 474-0642

*State Archives:*
New York State Archives
11D40 Cultural Education Center
Albany, NY 12230
(518) 474-8955, (518) 473-9985 Fax

The New York Historical Society
Library Office
170 Central Park West
New York, NY 10024-5194
(212) 873-3400

NY State Historical Assn
Fennimore House, West Lake Rd.
PO Box 800
Cooperstown, NY 13326
(607) 547-2533

New York State Council of Genealogical Organizations
PO Box 2593
Syracuse, NY 13220-2593
(315) 262-2800

*Adoption Support Group:*
Birthparent Support Network
Liz Nowinski
669 Coney Island Ave.
Brooklyn, NY 11218
(718) 284-0666

Center for Reuniting Families
Dominic & Sarah Telesco
51 Burke Dr.
Buffalo, NY 14215
(716) 835-6387, (716) 835-1609 Fax

KinQuest, Inc., Barbara Ilardo
89 Massachusetts Ave.
Massapequa, NY 11758
(516) 541-7383, (718) 356-3674 Fax

Family Adoption Registry
(800) 345-5437
Website: *www.dfa.state.ny.us/adopt*

*Adoption Researcher:*
Adoption Crossroads, Nat'l Office
401 East 74th St #17D
New York, NY 10021
(212) 988-0110 Phone/Fax

State Adjutant General
330 Old Niskayuna Road
Latham, NY 12110-2224
(518) 786-4570

VA Regional Office
111 W. Huron Street
Buffalo, NY 14202
(800) 827-1000

VA Regional Office
245 W. Houston St
New York, NY 10014
(800) 827-1000

## NORTH CAROLINA

Area codes for state: 252, 336, 704, 828, 910, 919
State government information number: (919) 733-1110
State prison locator: (919) 716-3200
State website: *www.state.nc.us*

*Child Support Enforcement Office:*
Child Support Enforcement Section
100 East Six Forks Road
Raleigh, NC 27609
(800) 992-9457, (919) 571-4120

*State Vital Statistics:*
State Center for Health Statistics
Vital Records Branch
PO Box 29537
Raleigh, NC 27626-0537
(919) 733-4728

*State Driver Licenses:*
Department of Motor Vehicles
Drivers License Section
1100 New Bern Avenue
Raleigh, NC 27697
(919) 715-7000

*State Vehicle Titles/Registrations:*
Department of Motor Vehicles
Vehicle Registration Section
1100 New Bern Avenue
Raleigh, NC 27697
(919) 733-3025

NC Genealogical Society
PO Box 1492
Raleigh, NC 27602-1492

*State Archives:*
State Archives of North Carolina
Archival Services Branch
4614 Mail Service Center
Raleigh, NC 27699-4614
(919) 733-3952, (919) 733-1354 Fax
E-mail: archives@ncsl.dcr.state.nc.us

North Carolina Historical Societies
109 East Jones Street
Raleigh, NC 27601
(919) 733-7305

North Carolina Society of Historians
PO Box 848
Rockingham, NC 28379

*Adoption Support Group:*
Adoption Issues & Education
Amy Bergman
420 East 12th Street
Washington, NC 27889
(919) 975-1510

NC Adoption Connections
Lynn Giddens
PO Box 4153
Chapel Hill, NC 27515
(919) 967-5010, (919) 967-4010 Fax

*Adoption Researcher:*
Kinsolving Investigations
Christine Lee
PO Box 471921
Charlotte, NC 28247-1921
(704) 537-5919
(704) 846-5123 Fax
E-mail: mzchrislee@aol.com

State Adjutant General
4105 Reedy Creek Road
Raleigh, NC 27607-6410
(919) 664-6326

VA Regional Office
251 N. Main Street
Winston-Salem, NC 27155
(800) 827-1000

## NORTH DAKOTA

Area code for state: 701
State government information number: (701) 328-2000
State prison locator: (701) 328-6100
State website: *www.state.nd.us*

*Child Support Enforcement Office:*
ND Child Support Enforcement
PO Box 7190
Bismarck, ND 58507-7190
(800) 755-8530, (701) 328-3582
(701) 328-5497 Fax

*State Vital Statistics:*
State Department of Health
Vital Records
600 E. Boulevard Ave, 1st Floor
Bismarck, ND 58505-0200
(701) 328-2000, (701) 328-1850 Fax
*Divorce decrees are county records.

*State Driver Licenses:*
Department of Transportation
Driver License & Traffic Safety Div.
608 E. Boulevard Avenue
Bismarck, ND 58505-0700
(701) 328-2725

*State Vehicle Titles/Registrations:*
Department of Transportation
Records Section/Motor Vehicles Div.
608 E. Boulevard Avenue
Bismarck, ND 58505-0700
(701) 328-2725

*State Archives:*
State Historical Society
North Dakota Heritage Center
612 E. Boulevard Avenue
Bismarck, ND 58505-0830
(701) 328-2666, (701) 328-3710 Fax
E-mail: archives@state.nd.us

State Historical Society of ND
North Dakota Heritage Center
612 East Boulevard Avenue
Bismarck, ND 58505
(701) 224-2668

Bismarck-Mandan Historical & Genealogical Society
PO Box 485
Bismarck, ND 58501
(701) 223-2929

Adjutant General
PO Box 5511, Fraine Bks
Bismarck, ND 58502-5511
(701) 224-5100

VA Regional Office
2101 Elm Street
Fargo, ND 58102
(800) 827-1000

## OHIO

Area codes for state: 216, 330, 419, 440, 513, 614, 740, 937
State government information number: (614) 466-2000
State prison locator: (614) 752-1159
State website: *www.state.oh.us*

*Child Support Enforcement Office:*
Family Assistance & Child Support
30 E. Broad St, 32nd Floor
Columbus, OH 43266-0423
(800) 686-1556, (614) 466-6282
(614) 466-2815 Fax

*State Vital Statistics:*
Ohio Department of Health
Vital Statistics Unit
PO Box 15098
Columbus, OH 43215-0098
(614) 466-2531
*www.odh.state.oh.us/Birth/birthmain.htm*

*State Driver License:*
Bureau of Motor Vehicles
1970 West Broad Street
Columbus, OH 43223
(614) 752-7600, (614) 752-7681

*State Vehicle Titles/Registrations:*
Bureau of Motor Vehicles
1970 West Broad Street
Columbus, OH 43223
(614) 752-7800

*State Archives:*
Ohio Historical Society
Research Services Dept.
1982 Velma Avenue
Columbus, OH 43211-2497
(614) 297-2510, (614) 297-2546 Fax

Ohio Genealogical Society
Library
34 Sturges Avenue
PO Box 2625
Mansfield, OH 44906-0625
(419) 522-9077

*Adoption Support Group:*
Birthmothers Support Group
Berta Yenney
856 Pine Needles Drive
Centerville, OH 45458
(513) 436-0593

Adoption Network Cleveland
Betsie Norris
291 East 222nd Street, #229
Cleveland, OH 44123
(216) 261-1511
(216) 261-1164 Fax
E-mail: bln2@po.cwru.edu

*Adoption Researcher:*
Janet Huddleston-ISC
3230 Nidover Dr.
Akron, OH 44312
(216) 699-2082

State Adjutant General
2825 Dublin-Granville Road
Columbus, OH 43235-2712
(614) 889-7040

VA Regional Office
1240 E. 9th Street
Cleveland, OH 44199
(800) 827-1000

## OKLAHOMA

Area codes for state: 405, 580, 918
State government information number: (405) 521-2011
State prison locator: (405) 425-2624
State website: *www.state.ok.us*

Child Support Enforcement
Capitol Station
PO Box 53552
Oklahoma City, OK 73152
(800) 522-2922, (405) 522-5871
(405) 522-2753 Fax

*State Vital Statistics:*
State Department of Health
Vital Records Service
1000 NE 10th Street
Oklahoma City, OK 73117
(405) 271-4040
*Divorce/marriage are county records.

*State Driver Licenses:*
Department of Public Safety
Drivers Record Services
PO Box 11415
Oklahoma City, OK 73136-0415
(405) 425-2000

*State Vehicle Titles/Registrations:*
Oklahoma Tax Commission
Motor Vehicle Division Research
2501 N. Lincoln Blvd.
Oklahoma City, OK 73194
(405) 521-3214

*State Archives:*
Libraries Department
Archives & Records Office
200 N.E. 18th Street
Oklahoma City, OK 73105-3298
(405) 521-2502, (405) 525-7804 Fax

Oklahoma Historical Society
Library Resources Div.
Wiley Post Historical Bldg
2101 N. Lincoln Blvd
Oklahoma City, OK 73105-4915
(405) 521-2491, (405) 525-3272 Fax

Genealogical Institute of OK
3813 Cashion Place
Oklahoma City, OK 73112

Federation of Oklahoma
Genealogical Societies
PO Box 26151
Oklahoma City, OK 73126

Oklahoma Genealogical Society
PO Box 12986
Oklahoma City, OK 73157-2986

*Adoption Support Group:*
Shared Heartbeats
Sue Scott
PO Box 12125
Oklahoma City, OK 73157
(405) 943-4500

*Adoption Researcher:*
AR Adoption Connection
Jenny Kolp
Route 1, Box 135-54
Roland, OK 74954

State Adjutant General
3501 Military Circle, NE
Oklahoma City, OK 73111-4398
(405) 425-8203

VA Regional Office
125 S. Main Street
Muskogee, OK 74401
(800) 827-1000

Veterans Memorial Building
PO Box 53067
Oklahoma City, OK 73152
(405) 521-3684, (405) 521-6533 Fax

## OREGON

Area codes for state: 503, 541
State government information number: None available.
State prison locator: (503) 373-1595
State website: *www.state.or.us*

Child Support Enforcement Office
1495 Edgewater St NW, #170
Salem, OR 97304
(800) 850-0228, (503) 986-6090
(503) 986-6158 Fax

*State Vital Statistics:*
Oregon Health Division
Vital Records
PO Box 14050
Portland, OR 97293-0050
(503) 731-4108, (503) 234-8417 Fax

*State Driver Licenses:*
Driver and Motor Vehicle Services
1905 Lana Avenue
Salem, OR 97314
(503) 945-5000

*State Vehicle Titles/Registrations:*
Driver and Motor Vehicle Services
Record Services Unit
1905 Lana Avenue
Salem, OR 97314-2340
(503) 945-5000, 945-5425 Fax

*State Archives:*
Oregon State Archives
800 Summer Street, NE
Salem OR 97310
(503) 373-0701, (503) 373-0953 Fax

Oregon Historical Society
Historical Records Advisory Board
1200 SW Park Ave.
Portland, OR 97205-2483
(503) 222-1741, (503) 221-2035 Fax

Genealogical Forum of Oregon
Headquarters and Library
1410 SW Morrison St, Rm 812
Portland, OR 97205
(503) 227-2398

Genealogical Heritage Council
PO Box 628
Ashland, OR 97520-0021

Oregon Genealogical Society
PO Box 10306
Eugene, OR 97440-2306
(541) 746-7924

*Adoption Support Group:*
Oregon Adoptive Rights Assn.
Darlene Wilson
PO Box 882
Portland, OR 97207
(503) 235-3669
E-mail: mmxj31b@prodigy.com

*Adoption Researcher:*
Kathlyn Krautscheid, ISC
PO Box 7271
Aloha, OR 97007
(503) 645-2524

State Adjutant General
1776 Militia Way NE
Salem, OR 97309-5047
(503) 945-3939

VA Regional Office
1220 S.W. 3rd Avenue
Portland, OR 97204
(800) 827-1000

## PENNSYLVANIA

Area codes for state: 215, 267, 412, 484, 570, 610, 717, 724, 814
State government information number: (717) 787-2121
State Prison Locator: (717) 730-2721
State website: *www.state.pa.us*

Bureau of Child Support Enforcement
PO Box 8018
Harrisburg, PA 17105-8018
(800) 932-0211
(717) 787-3672
(717) 787-9706 Fax

*State Vital Statistics:*
State Department of Health
Division of Vital Records
PO Box 1528
New Castle, PA 16101
(724) 656-3100
*Divorce/marriage are county records.

*Driver Licenses/Titles & Registrations:*
Department of Transportation
1101-1125 South Front Street
Harrisburg, PA 17104
(717) 391-6190
(800) 932-4600

*State Archives:*
Historical & Museum Commission
State Archives
350 North Street
Harrisburg, PA 17120-0090
(717) 787-3281
(717) 783-4822 Fax

Heritage Society of Pennsylvania
PO Box 146
Laughlintown, PA 15655

Friends of PA Historical
and Museum Commission
PO Box 11466
Harrisburg, PA 17108-1466
(717) 783-2618

PA Historical Association
Penn State, Harrisburg
Crags Building
777 West Harrisburg Pike
Middletown, PA 17057-4898
(717) 774-4829

Historical Society of PA
1300 Locust Street
Philadelphia, PA 19107-5699
(215) 545-0391

Genealogical Society of PA
1300 Locust Street
Philadelphia, PA 19107-5699
(215) 545-0391

*Adoption Support Group:*
Adoption Forum of Philadelphia
Brad Jones
525 S. 4th St. #3465
Philadelphia, PA 19147
(215) 238-1116
E-mail: jones547@pond.com

*Adoption Researcher:*
Pittsburgh Adoption Connection
Glenda Shay
37 Edgecliff Rd.
Carnegie, PA 15106
(412) 279-2511, (412) 429-0988
E-mail: G.Shay@aol.com
E-mail: xdmd56b@prodigy.com

*Adoption Registry:*
PA Adoption Reunion Registry
Karen Dulca
PO Box 20
Irwin, PA 15642
(412) 864-0531
E-mail: xdmd56a@prodigy.com

State Adjutant General
Dept. of Military Affairs
Annville, PA 17003-5002
(717) 861-8531

VA Regional Office
PO Box 19104
Philadelphia, PA 19104
(800) 827-1000

VA Regional Office
1000 Liberty Avenue
Pittsburgh, PA 15222
(800) 827-1000

## RHODE ISLAND

Area code for state: 401
State government information number: (401) 222-2000
State prison locator: (401) 464-5180
State website: *www.state.ri.us*

*Child Support Enforcement Office:*
RI Child Support Enforcement
77 Dorrance Street
Providence, RI 02903
(800) 638-KIDS, (401) 277-2409
(401) 277-6674 Fax

*State Vital Statistics:*
State Department of Health
Division of Vital Records
3 Capitol Hill, Room 101
Providence, RI 02908-5097
(401) 222-2811
*Divorce decrees are county records.

*State Driver Licenses:*
Driving Records Clerk
Operator Control
345 Harris Avenue
Providence, RI 02909
(401) 277-2994

*State Vehicle Titles/Registrations:*
Registry of Motor Vehicles
c/o Registration Files
Two Capital Hill
Providence, RI 02903
(401) 277-2064

*State Archives:*
Archives Public Records Admin.
337 Westminster St
Providence, RI 02903
(401) 222-2353
(401) 222-3199 Fax

RI State Historical Society
110 Benevolent St
Providence, RI 02906
(401) 331-8575

Rhode Island Genealogical Society
13 Countryside Drive
Cumberland, RI 02864-2601

State Adjutant General
Command Readiness Center
645 New London Ave.
Cranston, RI 02920-3097
(401) 457-4102

VA Regional Office
380 Westminster Mall
Providence, RI 02903
(800) 827-1000

## SOUTH CAROLINA

Area codes for state: 803, 843, 864
State government information number: (803) 734-1000
State prison locator: (803) 896-8500
State website: *www.state.sc.us*

Child Support Enforcement
PO Box 1446
Columbia, SC 29202
(800) 768-5858, (803) 737-5875
(803) 734-6073 Fax

*State Vital Statistics:*
Dept. of Health & Env. Control
Bureau of Vital Statistics
2600 Bull Street
Columbia, SC 29201
(803) 734-4830

*State Driver Licenses:*
Department of Public Safety
Driver Records Section
PO Box 1498
Columbia, SC 29216
(803) 737-4000

*State Vehicle Titles/Registrations:*
Division of Motor Vehicles
PO Box 1498
Columbia, SC 29216
(803) 737-1654

*State Archives:*
Archives & History Center
8301 Parklane Road
Columbia, SC 29223
(803) 896-6100, (803) 896-6198 Fax

South Carolina Historical Society
Fireproof Building
100 Meeting Street
Charleston, SC 29401
(803) 723-3225

South Carolina Historical Assn.
Francis Marion College
Florence, SC 29501

Confederation of South Carolina
Local Historical Societies
1430 Senate Street
Columbia, SC 29201
(803) 734-8577

South Carolina Genealogical Society
PO Box 16355
Greenville, SC 29606

*Adoption Support Group:*
Adoption Support Group of the CSRA
Alta McNatt
PO Box 7966
N. Augusta, SC 29861
(803) 279-0536

*Adoption Researcher:*
Missing Peace, Karne Conn
PO Box 507
Campobello, SC 29322
(803) 895-5385, (803) 895-1926 Fax
E-mail: deerwatson@aol.com

*Adoption Researcher:*
Adoption Reunion Connection
Liz White
PO Box 239
Moore, SC 29369
(864) 574-0681, (864) 574-6571 Fax
E-mail: VPQU48A@prodigy.com

State Adjutant General
1 National Guard Road
Columbia, SC 28201-3117
(803) 748-4228

VA Regional Office
1801 Assembly Street
Columbia, SC 29201
(800) 827-1000

## SOUTH DAKOTA

Area code for state: 605
State government information number: (605) 773-3011
State prison locator: (605) 367-5190
State website: *www.state.sd.us*

*Child Support Enforcement Office:*
SD Child Support Enforcement
700 Governors Drive
Pierre, SD 57501-2291
(605) 773-3641, (605) 773-5246 Fax

*State Vital Statistics:*
State Department of Health
Vital Records
600 E.. Capitol
Pierre, SD 57501-2536
(605) 773-4961

*State Driver Licenses:*
Division of Commerce & Regulation
Drivers License Program
118 W. Capitol Ave.
Pierre, SD 57501-2000
(605) 773-3018

*State Vehicle Titles/Registrations:*
Division of Motor Vehicles
Information Section
445 W. Capitol Avenue
Pierre, SD 57501-3185
(605) 773-5335

*State Archives:*
SD State Archives
900 Governors Drive
Pierre, SD 57501-2217
(605) 773-3804
(605) 773-6041 Fax
E-mail: Archref@state.sd.us

SD Genealogical Society
Rt. 2, Box 10
Burke, SD 57523
(605) 835-9364

State Adjutant General
2823 W. Main Street
Rapid City, SD 57702-8186
(605) 399-6710

VA Regional Office
2501 W. 22nd Street
Sioux Falls, SD 57115
(800) 827-1000

## TENNESSEE

Area codes for state: 423, 615, 865, 901, 931
State government information number: (615) 741-3011
State prison locator: (615) 741-2733
State website: *www.state.tn.us*

TN Child Support Enforcement
Dept of Human Services
Citizens Plaza Building
400 Deadrock Street
Nashville, TN 37248-7400
(800) 874-0530, (615) 313-4880
(615) 532-2791 Fax

*State Vital Statistics:*
TN Department of Health
Vital Records
Central Services Bldg.
421 5th Ave. N.
Nashville, TN 37247-0450
(615) 741-1763

*State Driver Licenses:*
Department of Safety
Driving License & Driving Records
1150 Foster Avenue
Nashville, TN 37249-1000
(615) 741-3954

*State Vehicle Titles/Registrations:*
Department of Motor Vehicles
44 Vantage Way, Suite 160
Nashville, TN 37243
(615) 741-3101

*State Archives:*
TN State Library & Archives
403 7th Avenue North
Nashville, TN 37243-0312
(615) 741-2764

Tennessee Historical Commission
2941 Lebanon Road
Nashville, TN 37243-0442
(615) 532-1550

Tennessee Historical Society
Ground Floor
War Memorial Building
300 Capital Boulevard
Nashville, TN 37243-0084
(615) 741-8934

Tennessee Genealogical Society
PO Box 111249
Memphis, TN 38111-1249
(901) 327-3273

*Adoption Support Group:*
Birthparents Search for Answers
Kathy Albaum
2750 Ward Rd.
Millington, TN 38053
E-mail: VEUC35A@prodigy.com

*Adoption Researcher:*
F.A.I.T.H.
Nadeen Hart-ISC
181 1/2 West Sevier Ave
Kingsport, TN 37660
(423) 378-4679
E-mail: XKDL32A@prodigy.com

State Adjutant General
PO Box 41502
Nashville, TN 37201-1501
(615) 532-3106

VA Regional Office
1190 9th Avenue, South
Nashville, TN 37203
(800) 827-1000

## TEXAS

Area codes for state: 210, 214, 254, 281, 361, 409, 469, 512, 713, 806, 817, 830, 832, 903, 915, 940, 956, 972
State government information number: (512) 463-4630
State prison locator: (409) 295-6371
State website: *www.state.tx.us*

Texas Child Support Enforcement
Office of Attorney General
PO Box 12017
Austin, TX 78711-2017

*State Vital Statistics:*
Texas Department of Health
Bureau of Vital Statistics
PO Box 12040
Austin, TX 78711-2040
(512) 458-7111

*State Driver Licenses:*
Dept. of Public Safety
Driver Records Bureau
PO Box 149246
Austin, TX 78714-9246
(512) 424-2600

*State Vehicle Titles/Registrations:*
Department of Transportation
Vehicle Titles & Registration Div.
Austin, TX 78779-0001
(512) 465-7611

*State Archives:*
Library & Archives Commission
PO Box 12927
Austin, TX 78711
(512) 463-5480
E-mail: archinfo@tsl.state.tx.us

Texas State Historical Association
PO Box 12276, University Station
Austin, TX 78711-2276
(512) 463-6100, (512) 475-4872 Fax

Texas State Genealogical Society
2507 Tannehill
Houston, TX 77008-3052
(713) 864-6862

*Adoption Researcher:*
Orphan Voyage, Peggy Dorn
5811 South Minster
Houston, TX 77035
(713) 723-1762

*Adoption Support Group:*
Adoption Counseling & Search
Patricia Martinez Dorner
206 Lochaven
San Antonio, TX 78213
(210) 341-2070 Phone/Fax

*Adoption Researcher:*
Searchline of Texas
Pat Palmer
1516 Old Orchard Road
Irving, TX 75061
(214) 445-7005

State Adjutant General
PO Box 5218
Austin, TX 78763-5218
(512) 465-5031

VA Regional Office
6900 Almeda Road
Houston, TX 77030
(800) 827-1000

## UTAH

Area code for state: 435, 801
State government information number: (801) 538-3000
State prison locator: (801) 265-5571
State website: *www.state.ut.us*

Utah Child Support Enforcement
PO Box 45011
Salt Lake City, UT 84145-0011
(801) 538-8500, (801) 536-8509 Fax

*State Vital Statistics:*
State Department of Health
Bureau of Vital Records
PO Box 141012
Salt Lake City, UT 84114-1012
(801) 538-6105

*State Driver Licenses:*
Department of Public Safety
Drivers License & Driving Records
PO Box 30560
Salt Lake City, UT 84130-0560
(801) 965-4437

*State Vehicle Titles/Registrations:*
State Tax Commission
Motor Vehicle Records
1095 Motor Avenue
Salt Lake City, UT 84116
(801) 538-8300

*State Archives:*
State Archives & Records Service
PO Box 14121
State Capitol Archives Building
Salt Lake City, UT 84114-1021
(801) 538-3012, (801) 538-3354 Fax
E-mail: research@das.state.ut.us

Utah State Historical Society
Department of Community &
Economic Development
Division of State History
300 Rio Grande
Salt Lake City, UT 84101-1182
(801) 538-8700

Association of Utah Historians
1845 South 1800 East
Salt Lake City, UT 84108
(801) 533-7037

Utah Genealogical Association
PO Box 1144
Salt Lake City, UT 84110
(801) 262-7263, (801) 531-2091

*Adoption Researcher/Support Group:*
L.A.M.B.
Charlotte Staten
672 East 2025 South
Bountiful, UT 84010
(801) 298-8520

State Adjutant General
PO Box 1776
Draper, UT 84020-1776
(801) 576-3616

VA Regional Office
125 S. State Street
Salt Lake City, UT 84147
(800) 827-1000

## VERMONT

Area code for state: 802
State government information number: (802) 828-1110
State prison locator: (802) 241-2305
State website: *www.state.vt.us*

Child Support Enforcement Office
103 South Main Street
Waterbury, VT 05671-1901
(800) 622-4120, (802) 241-2313
(802) 244-1483 Fax

*State Vital Statistics:*
Vermont Department of Health
PO Box 70
Burlington, VT 05402
(802) 863-7275

*State Driver Licenses:*
Department of Motor Vehicles
State Office Building
120 State Street
Montpelier, VT 05601-0001
(802) 828-2000

*State Vehicle Titles/Registrations:*
Department of Motor Vehicles
Registration & License Info. Records
120 State Street
Montpelier, VT 05601-0001
(802) 828-2000

State Archives
Redstone Building
26 Terrace Street, Drawer 09
Montpelier, VT 05609-1101
(802) 828-2363
*http://vermont-archives.org*

Vermont Historical Society
Pavilion Office Building
109 State Street
Montpelier, VT 05609-0901
(802) 828-2291

Genealogical Society of Vermont
PO Box 422
Pittsford, VT 05763
(802) 483-2900

*Adoption Support Group:*
Marge Garfield
RR 1, Box 83
E. Calais, VT 05650
(802) 456-8850, (802) 456-8850 Fax
E-mail: beleaf4u@aol.com

*Adoption Researcher:*
Adoption Alliance of VT
Enoch Tompkins
107 Twin Oaks
S. Burlington, VT 05403
(802) 863-1727

State Adjutant General
Bldg #1, Camp Johnson
Colchester, VT 05446
(802) 654-0130

VA Regional Office
125 N. Main Street
White River Junction, VT 05009
(800) 827-1000

## VIRGINIA

Area codes for state: 540, 703, 757, 804
State government information number: (804) 786-0000
State prison locator: (804) 674-3000
State website: *www.state.va.us*

*Child Support Enforcement Office:*
Division of Social Services
730 East Broad Street
Richmond, VA 23219
(804) 692-1900
(804) 692-1405 Fax

*State Vital Statistics:*
State Department of Health
Office of Vital Records
PO Box 1000
Richmond, VA 23208-1000
(804) 225-5000

*State Driver Licenses:*
Department of Motor Vehicles
Records Request
PO Box 27412
Richmond, VA 23269
(804) 367-0538

*State Vehicle Titles/Registrations:*
Management Info. Administration
Vehicle Research Section
PO Box 27412
Richmond, VA 23269
(804) 367-6729

*State Archives:*
Archives Research Services
Library Building
800 E. Broad Street
Richmond, VA 23219-8000
(804) 692-3888

Virginia Historical Society
PO Box 7311
Richmond, VA 23211-0311
(804) 342-9677

Genealogical Research Institute of VA
PO Box 29178
Richmond, VA 23242-0178

Virginia Genealogical Society
5001 W. Broad St, #115
Richmond, VA 23230-3023
(804) 285-8954

*Adoption Support Group:*
Adoptees & Natural Parents Org.
Billie Quigley
949 Lacon Drive
Newport News, VA 23608
(804) 874-9091

*Adoption Researcher:*
Adoptees & Natural Parents Org.
Sandra Shaw
202 Old Landing Road
Yorktown, VA 23692
(804) 898-5432
E-mail: ros77@aol.com

State Adjutant General
501 E. Franklin Street
Richmond, VA 23218-2317
(804) 775-9116

VA Regional Office
210 Franklin Road, SW
Roanoke, VA 24011
(800) 827-1000

## WASHINGTON

Area codes for state: 206, 253, 360, 425, 509
State government information number: (360) 753-5000
State prison locator: (360) 753-1573
State website: *www.state.wa.us*

Child Support Enforcement Office:
Washington State Support Registry
712 Pear Street SE
PO Box 9008
Olympia, WA 98507-9008
(800) 922-4306, (360) 664-6900
(360) 664-5209 Fax

*State Vital Statistics:*
Department of Health
Center for Health Statistics
PO Box 9709
Olympia, WA 98507-9709
(360) 236-4313

*State Driver Licenses:*
Department of Licensing
Drivers Responsibility Division
PO Box 9909
Olympia, WA 98507-8500
(360) 902-3600

State Vehicle Titles/Registrations:
Department of Licensing
Vehicle Services
PO Box 9909
Olympia, WA 98507-8500
(360) 753-6990

*State Archives:*
Washington State Archives
PO Box 40238
Olympia, WA 98504-0238
(360) 753-5485, (360) 664-8814 Fax
E-mail: archives@secstate.wa.gov

Washington State Historical Society
1911 Pacific Avenue
Tacoma, WA 98402
(253) 798-5901, (253) 272-9518 Fax

WA State Genealogical Society
PO Box 1422
Olympia, WA 98507-1422

*Adoption Support Group:*
WARM
Carol Arkinson
245 Fourth Street #201A
Bremerton, WA 98337
(360) 377-0341, (360) 373-9053 Fax

*Adoption Researcher:*
American Adoption Congress
Carole A. VandenBos
14435 22nd Avenue SW
Seattle, WA 98166
(206) 244-5134, (206) 244-5134 Fax
E-mail: GWGS04A@prodigy.com

*Adoption Researcher:*
Janet Mackey
North 1114 Locust Road
Spokane, WA 99206-4078
(509) 891-1876, (509) 926-1493 Fax
E-mail: BNBG46A@prodigy.com

State Adjutant General
Camp Murray
Tacoma, WA 98430-5000
(253) 512-8201

VA Regional Office
915 2nd Avenue
Seattle, WA 98174
(800) 827-1000

## WEST VIRGINIA

Area code for state: 304
State government information number: (304) 558-3456
State prison locator: (304) 558-2036
State website: *www.state.wv.us*

*Child Enforcement Office:*
Bureau for Child Support
State Capitol Complex
Building 6, Room 817
Charleston, WV 25305
(800) 249-3778, (304) 558-3780
(304) 558-4092 Fax

*State Vital Statistics:*
Dept. of Health & Human Resources
Vital Registration Office
350 Capitol Street, Rm 165
Charleston, WV 25301-3701

*State Driver Licenses:*
Division of Motor Vehicles
1900 Kanawha Blvd. E.
Charleston, WV 25305
(304) 558-3900

*State Vehicle Titles/Registrations:*
Division of Motor Vehicles
Titles and Registration Division
1608 Washington St. E.
Charleston, WV 25317
(304) 558-0282

*State Archives:*
WV State Archives
Archives and History Library
1900 Kanawha Blvd.
Charleston, WV 25305-0300
(304) 558-0220, (304) 558-2779 Fax

WV Historical Society
Division of Culture and History
The Cultural Center
PO Box 5220
Charleston, WV 25361-0220

WV Genealogical Society
PO Box 249
Elkview, WV 25071-0249

*Adoption Support Group:*
Loretta Hopson
826 Honaker Lane
Charleston, WV 25312
(304) 984-0305

*Adoption Researcher:*
Karl Slater
3728 Sissonville Drive
Charleston, WV 25312
(304) 343-3641

State Adjutant General
1703 Coonskin Drive
Charleston, WV 25311-1085
(304) 561-6300

VA Regional Office
640 Fourth Avenue
Huntington, WV 25701
(800) 827-1000

## WISCONSIN

Area codes for state: 262, 414, 608, 715, 920
State government information number: (608) 266-2211
State prison locator: (608) 266-2097
State website: *www.state.wi.us*

Child Support Enforcement Office
201 E. Washington Ave
GEF 1, Room 271-X
Madison, WI 53707
(608) 266-9909, (608) 267-2824 Fax

*State Vital Statistics:*
Dept. of Health & Family Services
Vital Records
PO Box 309
Madison, WI 53701-0309
(608) 266-1371

*State Driver Licenses:*
Department of Motor Vehicles
License Record Section
PO Box 7918
Madison, WI 53707
(608) 264-7060

*State Vehicle Titles/Registrations:*
Department of Transportation
Vehicle Records Section
PO Box 7911
Madison, WI 53707
(608) 266-3666

*State Archives:*
Wisconsin State Archives
Archives Reference
816 State Street
Madison, WI 53706
(608) 264-6400, (608) 264-6577 Fax
E-mail: archref@mail.shsw.wic.edu

State Historical Society of WI
816 State Street
Madison, WI 53706
(608) 264-6535, (608) 264-6460

Wisconsin State Genealogical Society
PO Box 5106
Madison, WI 53705-0106
(608) 325-2609

*Adoption Researcher:*
Carroll Duer
280 N. Campbell Rd, #D
Oshkosh, WI 54901
(414) 233-6487

*Adoption Support Group:*
Adoption Roots Traced
Mary Sue Wedle
N 6795 Hwy A #44
Lake Mills, WI 53551
(414) 648-2917 Phone/Fax
E-mail: mswedle@intaccess.com

State Adjutant General
3020 Wright Street
Madison, WI 53708-6111
608-242-3003

VA Regional Office
5000 W. National Ave. B-6
Milwaukee, WI 53295
(800) 827-1000

## WYOMING

Area code for state: 307
State government information number: (307) 777-7011
State prison locator: (307) 328-1441
State website: *www.state.wy.us*

Child Support Enforcement Registry
Hathaway Building, 3rd Floor
2300 Capitol Avenue
Cheyenne, WY 82002
(307) 777-6948, (307) 777-3693 Fax

*State Vital Statistics:*
Department of Health
Vital Records Services
Hathaway Building
Cheyenne, WY 82002
(307) 777-7591

*State Driver Licenses:*
WY Dept of Transportation
Drivers Services
5300 Bishop Blvd.
Cheyenne, WY 82009-3340
(307) 777-4800, (307) 777-4810
State Adjutant General
5500 Bishop Blvd
Cheyenne, Wy 82009-3320
(307) 772-5234

*State Vehicle Titles/Registrations:*
Dept of Transportation
Motor Vehicle License and Titles
5300 Bishop Blvd.
Cheyenne, WY 82009-3340
(307) 777-4709

*State Archives:*
Wyoming State Archives
Barrett Building
2301 Central Avenue
Cheyenne, WY 82002
(307) 777-7826, (307) 777-7044 Fax
E-mail: wyarchive@state.wy.us

Wyoming State Historical Society
Barrett State Office Building
2301 Central Avenue
Cheyenne, WY 82002
(307) 777-7015

VA Regional Office
2360 E. Pershing Blvd.
Cheyenne, WY 82001
(800) 827-1000

# Appendix B

## *National Archives Regional Facilities*

The National Archives and Records Administration (NARA) is part of the executive branch of the Federal government and is responsible for the maintenance and holdings of all Federal government agency records. The NARA website explains what is held where (*www.nara.gov*). Contact NARA's customer service center at (800) 234-8861.

### NARA National Records

Office of the Federal Register
Seventh & Pennsylvania Ave, NW
Washington, DC 20408-0001
E-mail: info@fedreg.nara.gov

National Archives and Records Administration
8601 Adelphi Rd
College Park, MD 20740-6001

Washington National Records Center (WNRC)
4205 Suitland Road
Washington, DC 20746-8001
(301) 457-7000
E-mail: center@suitland.nara.gov

National Personnel Records Center
Military Personnel Records
9700 Page Boulevard
St. Louis, MO 63132-5100
Records: U.S. military personnel and medical records.
E-mail: center@stlouis.nara.gov
*www.nara.gov/regional/mpr.html*

National Personnel Records Center
Civilian Records Facilty
111 Winnebago Street
St. Louis, MO 63118-4126
Records: Civil service personnel and medical records.
*www.nara.gov/regional/cpr.htm*

## National Archives Regional Centers

All the National Archives Regional Centers have the 1920 census (and prior), Revolutionary War records, federal court documents (for the area). Unlike the state historical/genealogical societies, the National Archives will not perform searches. You can visit their locations and search their records yourself or contact the Archives for a list of researchers. Local researchers usually charge an hourly fee.

National Archives, Northeast Region
10 Conte Drive
Pittsfield, MA 01201-8230
(413) 445-6885, 445-7599 Fax
E-mail: archives@pittsfield.nara.gov
*www.nara.gov/regional/pittsfie.html*

National Archives, Northeast Region
380 Trapelo Road
Waltham, MA 02452-6399
(781) 647-8104, 647-8088 Fax
E-mail: archives@waltham.nara.gov
*www.nara.gov/regional/boston.html*
Connecticut, Maine, Massachusetts, New Hampshire, Rhode Island, Vermont.

National Archives, Northeast Region
201 Varick Street
New York, NY 10014-4811
(212) 337-1300, 337-1306 Fax
E-mail: archives@newyork.nara.gov
*www.nara.gov/regional/newyork.html*
New Jersey, New York, Puerto Rico, Virgin Islands.

National Arhives, Mid-Atlantic Region
14700 Townsend Road
Philadelphia, PA 19154-1096
(215) 671-9027, 671-8001 Fax
E-mail: center@philfrc.nara.gov
*www.nara.gov/regional/philane.html*
Delaware, Maryland, Pennsylvania, Virginia, West Virginia.

National Archives, Mid-Atlantic Region
900 Market Street
Philadelphia, PA 19107-4292
(215) 597-3000, 597-2303 Fax
E-mail: archives@philarch.nara.gov
*www.nara.gov/regional/philacc.html*

National Archives, Southeast Region
1557 St. Joseph Avenue
East Point, GA 30344-2593
(404) 763-7474, 763-7059 Fax
E-mail: center@atlanta.nara.gov
*www.nara.gov/regional/atlanta.html*
Alabama, Florida, Georgia, Kentucky, Mississippi, North Carolina, South Carolina, Tennessee.

National Archives, Great Lakes Region
3150 Springboro Road
Dayton, OH 45439-1883
(937) 225-2852, 225-7236 Fax
E-mail: center@dayton.nara.gov
*www.nara.gov/regional/dayton/html*
Indiana, Michigan, Ohio.

National Archives, Great Lakes Region
7358 South Pulaski Road
Chicago, IL 60629-5898
(773) 581-7816, (312) 353-1294 Fx
E-mail: archives@chicago.nara.gov
*www.nara.gov.regional/chicago.html*
Illinois, Indiana, Michigan, Ohio, Wisconsin.

National Archives, Central Plains Region
2312 East Bannister Road
Kansas City, MO 64131-3011
(816) 926-6272, 926-6982 Fax
Email: archives@kansascity.nara.gov
*www.nara.gov/regional/kansas.html*
Iowa, Kansas, Missouri, Nebraska

National Archives, Central Plains Region
200 Space Center Drive
Lee's Summit, MO 64064-1182
(816) 478-7079, 478-7625 Fax
E-mail: center@kccave.nara.gov
*www.nara.gov/regional/leesumit.html*
New Jersey, New York, Puerto Rico, Virgin Islands, Dept. of Veterans Affairs, and Immigration & Naturalization Service Offices, nationwide.

National Archives, Southwest Region
501 West Felix Street, Bldg #1
Fort Worth, TX 76115-3405
(817) 334-5525, 334-5621 Fax
E-mail: archives@ftworth.nara.gov
*www.nara.gov/regional/ftworth.html*
Arkansas, Louisiana, Oklahoma, Texas.

National Archives, Rocky Mountain Region
Building 48, Denver Federal Center
West 6th Avenue and Kipling Street
Denver, Colorado 80225-0001
(303) 236-0817, 236-9297 Fax
E-mail: archives@denver.nara.gov
*www.nara.gov/regional/denver.html*
Colorado, Montana, New Mexico, North Dakota, South Dakota, Utah, Wyoming.

National Archives, Pacific Region
24000 Avila Road
Laguna Niguel, CA 92677-3497
(949) 360-2641, 360-2624 Fax
E-mail: archives@lunga.nara.gov
*www.nara.gov/regional/laguna.html*
Arizona, southern California, Nevada (only Clark County).

National Archives, Pacific Region
1000 Commodore Drive
San Bruno, CA 94066-2350
(650) 876-9009, 876-9233 Fax
Microfilm: (650) 876-9009
E-mail: archives@sanbruno.nara.gov
*www.nara.gov/regional/sanfranc.html*
Northern California, Hawaii, Nevada (except Clark county), American Samoa, Trust Territory of Pacific Islands.

National Archives, Pacific Alaska Region
6125 Sand Point Way, NE
Seattle, WA 98115-7999
(206) 526-6501, 526-6575 Fax
E-mail: archives@seattle.nara.gov
*www.nara.gov/regional/seattle.html*
Idaho, Oregon, Washington

National Archives, Pacific Alaska Region
654 West Third Avenue
Anchorage, AK 99501-2145
(907) 271-2443,271-2442 Fax
E-mail: archives@alaska.nara.gov
*www.nara.gov/regional/anchorage.html*
Alaska.

# Appendix C

## Freedom of Information Act Request

This is a sample letter for contacting the armed forces and federal agencies concerning a FOIA request:

[Date]
[Agency Head or FOIA Officer]
[Name of Agency]
[Address]

TO WHOM IT MAY CONCERN:

Under the Freedom of Information Act, 5 USC, subsection 532, I am requesting access to, or copies of [identify the records as clearly and specifically as possible].

If there are any fees for copying or searching the records please let me know before you fulfill my request [or, please supply the records without informing me of the cost if the fees do not exceed $____, which I agree to pay].

[Optional:] I am requesting this information because [state the reason(s) if you think it will help you obtain the information].

If you deny all or any part of this request, please cite each specific exemption that justifies your refusal to release the information and notify me of appeal procedures available under the law.

[Optional:] If you have any questions about this request, you may telephone me at [home phone] or at [office phone].

Sincerely,

[Your name]

[Address]

## *Individual Data Worksheet*

Complete legal name, nicknames, maiden name, previous married names, and aliases ______________________________________________

______________________________________________

______________________________________________

Social Security number ______________________________

Date of birth ______________________________

Place of birth ______________________________

Parents' names ______________________________

______________________________________________

Spouse and former spouse's name(s) ______________________________

______________________________________________

Names of brothers and sisters ______________________________

______________________________________________

Names of other relatives ______________________________

______________________________________________

______________________________________________

Children's names and addresses ______________________________

______________________________________________

Previous addresses ______________________________

______________________________________________

______________________________________________

______________________________________________

Previous telephone number(s) ______________________________

Military service number ______________________________

VA claim number/VA insurance number ______________________________

______________________________________________

Branch of military service ______________________________

Dates of military service ______________________________

Unit or ship assigned ______________________________

Installation or base assigned ______________________________

Assignments in Vietnam, Korea, etc. ______________________________

Rank or rating (if not known, officer or enlisted) ______________________________

Membership in veterans and military reunion organizations ______________

______________________________________________

Membership in the reserve or National Guard; units/dates of assignment:

______________________________________________

Real estate owned ______________________________

______________________________________________

Automobiles, motorcycles and boats owned/state in which registered

___

___

Elementary, high schools, colleges and universities attended, locations and dates ___

___

___

Previous employment/dates and locations ___

___

___

___

Church or synagogue affiliation ___

Union membership ___

Professional membership/licenses ___

Lodges, fraternal and service organization membership ___

___

Physical description: height, weight, color of hair and eyes, tattoos, scars, etc. (obtain photos) ___

___

___

Hunting, boating or fishing licenses ___

___

Pilot, amateur radio, driver and motorcycle licenses ___

___

Names, addresses and telephone numbers of friends and fellow employees

___

___

___

___

Hobbies, talents and avocations ___

___

Political party affiliation and voter's registration ___

Foreign and national travel history ___

___

Dates and places of bankruptcy ___

Miscellaneous information ___

___

___

___

## INSTRUCTIONS for Standard Form 180 (next 2 pages)

1. **Information needed to locate records**. Certain identifying information is necessary to determine the location of an individual's record of military service. Please try to answer each item on this form. If you do not have and cannot obtain the information for an item, show "NA," meaning the information is "not available." Include as much of the requested information as you can.

2. **Restrictions on release of information**. Release of information is subject to restrictions imposed by the military services consistent with Department of Defense regulations and the provisions of the Freedom of Information Act (FOIA) and the Privacy Act of 1974. The service member (either past or present) or the member's legal guardian has access to almost any information contained in that member's own record. Others requesting information from military personnel/health records must have the release authorization in Section III of this form signed by the member or legal guardian, but if the appropriate signature cannot be obtained, only limited types of information can be provided. If the former member is deceased, surviving next of kin may, under certain circumstances, be entitled to greater access to a deceased veteran's records than a member of the public. The next of kin may be any of the following: unremarried surviving spouse, father, mother, son, daughter, sister, or brother. Employers and others needing proof of military service are expected to accept the information shown on documents issued by the military service departments at the time a service member separated.

3. **Where reply may be sent.** The reply may be sent to the member or any other address designated by the member or other authorized requester.

4. **Charges for service**. There is no charge for most services provided to members or their surviving next of kin. A nominal fee is charged for certain types of service. In most instances service fees cannot be determined in advance. If your request involves a service fee, you will be notified as soon as that determination is made.

## PRIVACY ACT OF 1974 COMPLIANCE INFORMATION

Authority for collection of the information is 44 U.S.C. 2907, 3101, 3103, and E.O. 9397 of November 22, 1943. Disclosure of the information is voluntary. If the requested information is not provided, it may delay servicing your inquiry because the facility servicing the service member's record may not have all of the information needed to locate it. The purpose of the information on this form is to assist the facility servicing the records (see the address list) in locating the correct military service record(s) or information to answer your inquiry. This form is then filed in the requested military service record as a record of disclosure. The form may also be disclosed to Department of Defense components, the Department of Veterans Affairs, the Department of Transportation (Coast Guard), or the National Archives and Records Administration when the original custodian of the military health and personnel records transfers all or part of those records to that agency. If the service member was a member of the National Guard, the form may also be disclosed to the Adjutant General of the appropriate state, District of Columbia, or Puerto Rico, where he or she served.

Standard Form 180 (Rev. 3-99)
Prescribed by NARA (36 CFR 1228.162(a))
Authorized for local reproduction
Previous edition unusable
OMB No. 3095-0029 Expires 7/31/2002

**REQUEST PERTAINING TO MILITARY RECORDS**

To ensure the best possible service, please thoroughly review the instructions at the bottom before filling out this form. Please print clearly or type. If you need more space, use plain paper.

## SECTION I - INFORMATION NEEDED TO LOCATE RECORDS (Furnish as much as possible.)

| 1. NAME USED DURING SERVICE (Last, first, middle) | 2. SOCIAL SECURITY NO. | 3. DATE OF BIRTH | 4. PLACE OF BIRTH |
|---|---|---|---|
| | | | |

5. **SERVICE, PAST AND PRESENT** (For an effective records search, it is important that ALL service be shown below.)

| | BRANCH OF SERVICE | DATES OF SERVICE | | CHECK ONE | | SERVICE NUMBER DURING THIS PERIOD (If unknown, please write "unknown.") |
|---|---|---|---|---|---|---|
| | | DATE ENTERED | DATE RELEASED | OFFICER | ENLISTED | |
| a. ACTIVE SERVICE | | | | | | |
| | | | | | | |
| | | | | | | |
| b. RESERVE SERVICE | | | | | | |
| | | | | | | |
| c. NATIONAL GUARD | | | | | | |
| | | | | | | |

6. **IS THIS PERSON DECEASED?** If "YES" enter the date of death.
☐ NO ☐ YES ____________

7. **IS (WAS) THIS PERSON RETIRED FROM MILITARY SERVICE?**
☐ YES ☐ NO

## SECTION II - INFORMATION AND/OR DOCUMENTS REQUESTED

1. **REPORT OF SEPARATION** (DD Form 214 or equivalent) This contains information normally needed to verify military service. A copy may be sent to the veteran, the deceased veteran's next of kin, or other persons or organizations if authorized in Section III, below. NOTE: If more than one period of service was performed, even in the same branch, there may be more than one Report of Separation. Be sure to show EACH year that a Report of Separation was issued, for which you need a copy.

☐ An **UNDELETED** Report of Separation is requested for the year(s) ____________

This normally will be a copy of the full separation document including such sensitive items as the character of separation, authority for separation, reason for separation, reenlistment eligibility code, separation (SPD/SPN) code, and dates of time lost. An undeleted version is ordinarily required to determine eligibility for benefits.

☐ A **DELETED** Report of Separation is requested for the year(s) ____________

The following information will be deleted from the copy sent: authority for separation, reason for separation, reenlistment eligibility code, separation (SPD/SPN) code, and for separations after June 30, 1979, character of separation and dates of time lost.

2. **OTHER INFORMATION AND/OR DOCUMENTS REQUESTED** ____________

3. **PURPOSE** (OPTIONAL--An explanation of the purpose of the request is strictly voluntary. Such information may help the agency answering this request to provide the best possible response and will in no way be used to make a decision to deny the request.) ____________

## SECTION III - RETURN ADDRESS AND SIGNATURE

1. **REQUESTER IS**

☐ Military service member or veteran identified in Section I, above

☐ Legal guardian (must submit copy of court appointment)

☐ Next of kin of deceased veteran ____________ (relation)

☐ Other (specify) ____________

2. **SEND INFORMATION/DOCUMENTS TO**
(Please print or type. See instruction 3, below.)

Name

Street Apt.

City State ZIP Code

3. **AUTHORIZATION SIGNATURE REQUIRED** (See instruction 2, below.)
I declare (or certify, verify, or state) under penalty of perjury under the laws of the United States of America that the information in this Section III is true and correct.

Signature of requester (Please do not print.)

Date of this request Daytime phone ( )

E-mail address

**This form is available at *http://www.nara.gov/regional/mprsf180.html* on the National Archives and Records Administration (NARA) Web site.**

(See next page.)

# LOCATION OF MILITARY RECORDS

The various categories of military service records are described in the chart below. For each category there is a code number which indicates the address at the bottom of the page to which this request should be sent.

1. **Health and personnel records**. In most cases involving individuals no longer on active duty, the personnel record, the health record, or both can be obtained from the same location, as shown on the chart. However, some health records are available from the Department of Veterans Affairs (VA) Records Management Center (Code 11). A request for a copy of the health record should be sent to Code 11 if the person was discharged, retired, or released from active duty (separated) on or after the following dates: ARMY–October 16, 1992; NAVY–January 31, 1994; AIR FORCE and MARINE CORPS–May 1, 1994; COAST GUARD–April 1, 1998. Health records of persons on active duty are generally kept at the local servicing clinic, and usually are available from Code 11 a week or two after the last day of active duty.

2. **Records at the National Personnel Records Center**. Note that it takes at least three months, and often six or seven, for the file to reach the National Personnel Records Center (Code 14) in St. Louis after the military obligation has ended (such as by discharge). If only a short time has passed, please send the inquiry to the address shown for active or current reserve members. Also, if the person has only been released from active duty but is still in a reserve status, the personnel record will stay at the location specified for reservists. A person can retain a reserve obligation for several years, even without attending meetings or receiving annual training.

3. **Definitions and abbreviations**. DISCHARGED–the individual has no current military status; HEALTH–Records of physical examinations, dental treatment, and outpatient medical treatment received while in a duty status (does not include records of treatment while hospitalized); TDRL–Temporary Disability Retired List.

4. **Service completed before World War I**. The oldest records pertaining to military service veterans are at the National Archives, for service that was completed before the following dates: ARMY–enlisted, 11/1/1912, officer, 7/1/1917; NAVY–enlisted, 1/1/1886, officer, 1/1/1903; MARINE CORPS–1/1/1905; COAST GUARD–1/1/1898. National Archives Trust Fund (NATF) forms must be used to request these records. Obtain the forms by e-mail from *inquire@nara.gov* or write to the Code 6 address.

| BRANCH | CURRENT STATUS OF SERVICE MEMBER | WHERE TO WRITE ADDRESS CODE ▼ |
|---|---|---|
| AIR FORCE | Discharged, deceased, or retired with pay (See paragraph 1, above, if requesting health record.) | 14 |
| | Active (including National Guard on active duty in the Air Force), TDRL, or general officers retired with pay | 1 |
| | Reserve, retired reserve in nonpay status, current National Guard officers not on active duty in the Air Force, or National Guard released from active duty in the Air Force | 2 |
| | Current National Guard enlisted not on active duty in the Air Force | 13 |
| COAST GUARD | Discharged, deceased, or retired (See paragraph 1, above, if requesting health record.) | 14 |
| | Active, reserve, or TDRL | 3 |
| MARINE CORPS | Discharged, deceased, or retired (See paragraph 1, above, if requesting health record.) | 14 |
| | Individual Ready Reserve or Fleet Marine Corps Reserve | 5 |
| | Active, Selected Marine Corps Reserve, or TDRL | 4 |
| ARMY | Discharged, deceased, or retired (See paragraph 1, above, if requesting health record.) | 14 |
| | Reserve; or active duty records of current National Guard members who performed service in the U.S. Army before 7/1/72 | 7 |
| | Active enlisted (including National Guard on active duty in the U.S. Army) or TDRL enlisted | 9 |
| | Active officers (including National Guard on active duty in the U.S. Army) or TDRL officers | 8 |
| | Current National Guard enlisted not on active duty in Army (including records of Army active duty performed after 6/30/72) | 13 |
| | Current National Guard officers not on active duty in Army (including records of Army active duty performed after 6/30/72) | 12 |
| NAVY | Discharged, deceased, or retired (See paragraph 1, above, if requesting health record.) | 14 |
| | Active, reserve, or TDRL | 10 |

**ADDRESS LIST OF CUSTODIANS (BY CODE NUMBERS SHOWN ABOVE) - where to write/send this form**

|  |  |
|---|---|
| 1 | Air Force Personnel Center<br>HQ AFPC/DPSRP<br>550 C Street West, Suite 19<br>Randolph AFB, TX 78150-4721 |
| 2 | Air Reserve Personnel Center/DSMR<br>6760 E. Irvington Pl. #4600<br>Denver, CO 80280-4600 |
| 3 | Commander CGPC-Adm-3<br>U.S. Coast Guard<br>2100 2nd Street, S.W.<br>Washington, DC 20593-0001 |
| 4 | Headquarters U.S. Marine Corps<br>Personnel Management Support Branch<br>(MMSB-10)<br>2008 Elliot Road<br>Quantico, VA 22134-5030 |
| 5 | Marine Corps Reserve Support Command<br>(Code MMI)<br>15303 Andrews Road<br>Kansas City, MO 64147-1207 |
| 6 | National Archives & Records Admin.<br>Old Military and Civil Records (NWCTB-Military), Textual Services Division<br>700 Pennsylvania Ave., N.W.<br>Washington, DC 20408-0001 |
| 7 | Commander<br>U.S. Army Reserve Personnel Command<br>ATTN: ARPC-ALQ-B<br>1 Reserve Way<br>St. Louis, MO 63132-5200 |
| 8 | U.S. Total Army Personnel Command<br>200 Stoval Street<br>Alexandria, VA 22332-0400 |
| 9 | Commander USAEREC<br>Attn: PCRE-F<br>8899 E. 56th St.<br>Indianapolis, IN 46249-5301 |
| 10 | Naval Personnel Command<br>5720 Integrity Drive<br>Millington, TN 38055-3130 |
| 11 | Department of Veterans Affairs<br>Records Management Center<br>P.O. Box 5020<br>St. Louis, MO 63115-5020 |
| 12 | Army National Guard Readiness Center<br>NGB-ARP<br>111 S. George Mason Dr.<br>Arlington, VA 22204-1382 |
| 13 | The Adjutant General<br>(of the appropriate state, DC, or Puerto Rico) |
| 14 | National Personnel Records Center<br>(Military Personnel Records)<br>9700 Page Avenue<br>St. Louis, MO 63132-5100 |

# Appendix D

## *Social Security Number Allocations*

This section explains the meaning of the number groups within each Social Security number. Sometimes this information can be very helpful in a search.

The Social Security Administration was formed in 1933. Between 1933 and 1972, Social Security numbers (SSNs) were assigned at field offices in each state. Since 1973, Social Security numbers have been issued by the central office.

The Social Security number consists of nine digits. The first three digits are the area number. The middle two digits are the group number. The last four digits are the serial number.

*Example*: SSN 123-45-6789
123 = Area number
45 = Group number
6789 = Serial number

### Area Number

The area number identifies the state indicated in the original application. The chart below shows the first 3 digits (area number) of the Social Security numbers allocated to each state and U.S. possession.

| | |
|---|---|
| 001-003 | New Hampshire |
| 005-007 | Maine |
| 008-009 | Vermont |
| 010-034 | Massachusetts |
| 035-039 | Rhode Island |
| 040-049 | Connecticut |
| 050-134 | New York |
| 135-158 | New Jersey |
| 159-211 | Pennsylvania |
| 212-220 | Maryland |
| 221-222 | Delaware |
| 223-231, 691-699* | Virginia |
| 232-236 | West Virginia |
| 232, 237-246, 681-690* | North Carolina |

| | |
|---|---|
| 247-251, 654-658* | South Carolina |
| 252-260, 667-675* | Georgia |
| 261-267, 589-595 | Florida |
| 268-302 | Ohio |
| 303-317 | Indiana |
| 318-361 | Illinois |
| 362-386 | Michigan |
| 387-399 | Wisconsin |
| 400-407 | Kentucky |
| 408-415, 756-763* | Tennessee |
| 416-424 | Alabama |
| 425-428, 587, 588*, 752-755* | Mississippi |
| 429-432, 676-679* | Arkansas |
| 433-439, 659-665* | Louisiana |
| 440-448 | Oklahoma |
| 449-467, 627-645 | Texas |
| 468-477 | Minnesota |
| 478-485 | Iowa |
| 486-500 | Missouri |
| 501-502 | North Dakota |
| 503-504 | South Dakota |
| 505-508 | Nebraska |
| 509-515 | Kansas |
| 516-517 | Montana |
| 518-519 | Idaho |
| 520 | Wyoming |
| 521-524, 650-653* | Colorado |
| 525, 585, 648-649* | New Mexico |
| 526-527, 600-601 | Arizona |
| 528-529, 646-647* | Utah |
| 530, 680* | Nevada |
| 531-539 | Washington |
| 540-544 | Oregon |
| 545-573, 602-626* | California |
| 574 | Alaska |
| 575-576, 750-751* | Hawaii |
| 577-579 | District of Columbia |
| 580 | Virgin Islands |
| 580-584, 596-599 | Puerto Rico |
| 586 | Guam |
| 586 | American Samoa |
| 586 | Philippine Islands |
| 700-728** | Railroad Board |

*Some of these numbers may not yet be issued.

**700-728 RRB (Railroad Board). Issuance of these numbers to railroad employees was discontinued July 1, 1963.

*Note*: The same area number, when shown more than once, means that certain numbers have been transferred from one state to another, or that an area number has been divided for use among certain geographic locations.

Area numbers range from 001 through 587, 589 through 649, and 700 through 728. Social Security numbers containing area numbers other than these are not valid.

Prior to converting from service numbers to Social Security numbers as a mean of identification, the military assigned dummy Social Security numbers to individuals who did not have them hen they entered the service. These dummy area numbers range from 900 through 999 and appear on some military orders and unit rosters in the late 1960s and early 1970s. The dummy numbers were later replaced with valid Social Security numbers.

## Group Number

As we have seen, the first three digits indicate the area (or state) of the Social Security number. Within each area, group numbers (the middle two digits) are allocated. These numbers range from 01 to 99, but are not assigned in consecutive order. For administrative reasons, the first group numbers issued are the odd numbers from 01 through 09. Then even numbers from 10 through 98 are issued. After all even numbers in group 98 of a particular area have been issued, the even numbers 02 through 08 are used, followed by odd numbers 11 through 99 as shown:

| | |
|---|---|
| Odd | 01, 03, 05, 07, 09 |
| Even | 10 through 98 |
| Even | 02, 04, 06, 08 |
| Odd | 11 through 99 |

The chart below shows the highest group number allocated for each area number as of February, 1997.

| | | | | | |
|---|---|---|---|---|---|
| 001-002 | 90 | 035-039 | 64 | 135-144 | 02 |
| 003 | 88 | 040-043 | 96 | 145-158 | 98 |
| 004-007 | 96 | 044-049 | 94 | 159-200 | 76 |
| 008-023 | 80 | 050-081 | 86 | 201-211 | 74 |
| 024-034 | 78 | 082-134 | 84 | 212-214 | 49 |

| | | | | | |
|---|---|---|---|---|---|
| 215-220 | 47 | 433 | 95 | 575 | 77 |
| 221-222 | 88 | 434-439 | 93 | 576 | 75 |
| 223-229 | 77 | 440-446 | 08 | 577 | 29 |
| 230-231 | 75 | 447-448 | 06 | 578-579 | 27 |
| 232 | 45 | 449-467 | 99 | 580 | 31 |
| 233-236 | 43 | 468 | 33 | 581-585 | 99 |
| 237-239 | 85 | 469-477 | 31 | 586 | 29 |
| 240-246 | 83 | 478-485 | 25 | 587 | 79 |
| 247-251 | 99 | 486-491 | 13 | 589-592 | 65 |
| 252-259 | 97 | 492-500 | 11 | 593-595 | 63 |
| 260 | 95 | 501-502 | 13 | 596-599 | 52 |
| 261-267 | 99 | 503 | 27 | 600 | 65 |
| 268-274 | 02 | 504 | 25 | 601 | 63 |
| 275-302 | 98 | 505-506 | 37 | 602-620 | 94 |
| 303 | 19 | 507-508 | 35 | 621-626 | 92 |
| 304-317 | 17 | 509-515 | 13 | 627-628 | 56 |
| 318-357 | 92 | 516 | 31 | 629-645 | 54 |
| 358-361 | 90 | 517 | 29 | 646 | 34 |
| 362-367 | 21 | 518 | 51 | 647 | 32 |
| 368-386 | 19 | 519 | 49 | 648-649 | 10 |
| 387-399 | 15 | 520 | 37 | 650 | 03 |
| 400-402 | 51 | 521-529 | 99 | 651-654 | 01 |
| 403-407 | 49 | 530 | 97 | 700-723 | 18 |
| 408-412 | 81 | 531-534 | 37 | 724 | 28 |
| 413-415 | 79 | 535-539 | 35 | 725-726 | 18 |
| 416 | 47 | 540 | 51 | 727 | 10 |
| 417-424 | 45 | 541-544 | 49 | 728 | 14 |
| 425-428 | 81 | 545-573 | 99 | | |
| 429-432 | 91 | 574 | 23 | | |

### Serial Number

Within each group, the serial numbers (last four digits of the Social Security number) run consecutively from 0001 through 9999.

# Appendix E

## *Locator Services*

### The Nationwide Locator

The Nationwide Locator is a professional locator service that performs computer searches to provide names, addresses and other important information to the public. They provide this information to heir searchers, attorneys, private investigators, collection agencies, reunion planners and individuals seeking information about friends or relatives. Their data is obtained from highly accurate and reasonably priced databases that contain information on 160+ million people.

When they first start out, beginning searchers may want to contact the Nationwide Locator to do a few searches. However, more serious searchers should obtain the computer access packages mentioned on page 241.

Following are the types of searches the Locator provides:

#### Social Security Search

Provide a name and Social Security number (SSN) and receive the person's most current reported address, date reported, and all previous reported addresses (if the SSN is contained in a national credit file). If a report of death has been submitted, it will be listed. $40 per SSN for a nationwide search.

#### Address Update

Provide a name and last known address (not over ten years old) and receive the most current reported address and the names and telephone numbers of five neighbors. $40 per name submitted.

#### National Surname Search

Provide a first name, middle initial and last name and a

national telephone directory will be used to provide the names, addresses and listed telephone numbers of everyone in the nation with a matching name. $40 per name.

**Date of Birth Search**

Provide first and last name, approximate date or year of birth and Social Security number (if known) and receive all matching names, city, and state of residence. May be able to provide street address and phone number. $95 per name and date of birth submitted.

**Social Security Death Index Search**

Provide either the name and date of birth, name and Social Security number, or name only and receive a list of people who are deceased, their SSN, date of birth, and the date and place of death as reported by the Social Security Administration. $40 per name.

Information will be provided to you within 24 hours of receipt, and will be returned by mail—or by fax, if requested. Volume discounts are available. Prices are subject to change without notice. Other specialized searches are available.

If you would like the Nationwide Locator to perform any of these searches for you, please write or fax the information required to the address or fax number listed at the bottom of the next page. Please include the following:

- Payment in full: check, money order or credit card. If using Visa, MasterCard or American Express, please include your card number, the expiration date, the amount charged, and your signature.
- Your name.
- Your phone number.
- Your address, including city, state and zip code.
- Fax number, if information is to be returned by fax.

## Computer Access Programs

The Nationwide Locator also markets a computer access program to locate missing people. The NIS program (see below) is used by heir searchers, private investigators, collection agencies, attorneys, reunion planners, and others who are searching for a large number of people.

The access package includes these categories of searches:

- Social Security trace
- Social Security number retrace (criss-cross)
- Name and date of birth search
- Postal forwarding
- Commercial credit
- Asset searches
- Motor vehicle registration traces
- Drivers license traces
- Criminal history
- Worker's compensation
- Numerous other on-line searches

The cost of each search varies. Most searches give instant on-line results, while some searches may take 3–5 days. You do not need a computer to use this program. It can be accessed by phone, fax or mail.

The NIS On-Line Information Service is user-friendly, menu-driven, available 24 hours a day and accessible by phone, mail, fax and e-mail. The cost of the NIS On-line Information Services is $395. You can be on-line within 3–5 days. For a brochure, write or fax:

The Nationwide Locator
PO Box 17118
Spartanburg, SC 29301
(864) 595-0813 Fax

## Obtaining Military Records

The U.S. Locator Service (not affiliated with the federal government) can quickly obtain records from the National Personnel Records Center and the Army Reserve Personnel Center in St. Louis, Missouri. All requests are properly prepared and hand-carried to the appropriate Center, thus assuring that you will receive the records in the quickest manner possible. The following records may be obtained:

- Certified copies of *Report of Separation (DD 214)* for anyone discharged or retired from the armed forces, and Army reservists who have been separated from active duty. Fee is $60. Allow 4-6 weeks for delivery.

- A copy of the *complete military personnel and medical records* (every item in the file is copied) of an individual. This can only be provided to the veteran, or his next of kin if the veteran is deceased. This includes records of individuals who are retired from any armed forces, most individuals who are discharged and have no reserve obligation (all branches), and current members of the Army reserve. Copies of military records of individuals on active duty, current members of the Army National Guard and Air National Guard, current members of the Navy, Marine and Air Force reserves cannot be obtained because these records are not at the NPRC. Fee is $110.

*Note*: Requests for DD 214 and military records are made with the authorization form shown on the page 244. It must be completed and signed by the veteran, or his next of kin if deceased. Please include proof of death (e.g., death certificate, obituary or funeral card).

- Certified copies of complete military personnel and medical records may also be obtained for attorneys and private investigators in four to six weeks for court cases. A court order signed by a federal or state judge is required. A sample of how the court order should be worded will be mailed or faxed upon request. Fee is $200.

- Organizational records can also be obtained. Write for further details.

All fees are for research and in the event the records requested are not available or were destroyed, the fee is not refundable. All requests must be prepaid and all information concerning the request should be included. All orders are shipped by first class mail but may be shipped overnight for an additional fee of $13. Checks should be made payable to U.S. Locator Service (not affiliated with the federal government) or you may make payment by credit card. For additional information or to order records, mail or fax authorization to:

U.S. Locator Service
PO Box 140194
St. Louis, MO 63114-0194
(314) 423-0860
*www.uslocatorservice.com*

Please use authorization form on next page.

# Military Records Authorization

I request and authorize that representatives of U.S. Locator Service be allowed to review my military and/or civilian service personnel and medical records, and/or auxiliary records in the same manner as if I presented myself for this purpose. I specifically authorize the National Personnel Records Center, St. Louis, Missouri, or other custodians of my military records, to release to U.S. Locator Service a complete copy of my military personnel and related medical records.

I am willing that a photocopy and or fax of this authorization be considered as effective and valid as the original.

Signature ______________________________ Date ____________________

If veteran is deceased, date of death ______________________________

and relationship ________________________________________________

*<Instructions: Please type or print this authorization>*

Name ____________________________________________________________
Last First Middle initial

Street address ___________________________________ Apt. # _________

City ___________________________ State ______ Zip _______________

Social Security No. __________________ Phone No. _________________

Date of birth__________________ Place of birth ___________________

Service number __________________ Branch of service ____________

Dates of service _____________________________ Rank _____________

Current military status ( ) reserve, ( ) retired,

( ) separated with Army reserve obligation, ( ) none.

Please obtain: ( ) DD 214, ( ) complete military records,

( ) other ________________________________________________

Enclosed is: ( ) check, ( ) money order. Charge my ( ) Visa

( ) MasterCard, ( ) AMEX for $ _______________

Card No. ___________________________ Expir. date ________________

Signature _________________________________________________

Address where records are to be sent, if different from above:

________________________________________________________________

________________________________________________________________

# Appendix F

## *Helpful Publications*

Also see Federal Publications in Chapter 9.

*All In One Directory* by Gebby Press contains addresses, telephone numbers and fax numbers of almost every newspaper, including daily, weekly, business, trade, black and Hispanic newspapers. Also radio and television stations, and general and consumer magazines.

*The American Medical Directory* and *Directory of Medical Specialists*. These publications include names of physicians, their specialties, schooling, business addresses and various other information about doctors.

*Birthright: The Guide to Search and Reunion for Adoptees, Birthparents and Adoptive Parents*. An excellent resource for anyone searching for a birth parent, adoptive parent or a child given up for adoption.

*Directories in Print*. Lists the names and addresses of membership directories of hundreds of trade organizations and professional associations.

*Directory of American Libraries with Genealogical and Local History*. Provides a comprehensive listing of private and public libraries in the United States which have genealogical and local history sections. Published by Ancestry.

*Directory of Associations* and *Encyclopedia of Associations*. These two books contain addresses and telephone numbers of thousands of associations in the United States. Included are business oriented associations, veterans groups, professional and trade associations.

*Directory of Special Libraries and Information Centers*. Lists 15,000+ U.S. public libraries,19,000+ special libraries, archives, research libraries and information centers.

*Directory of Surnames*. Patrick Hanks and Flavia Hodges list alternate spellings of thousands of surnames. They also include origins and meanings of over 70,000 surnames.

*Directory of United States Libraries*. Complete list of U.S. libraries, published by the American Library Association.

*Foreign Service Lists*. These directories are published three times a year by the Department of State. They list field staffs of the U.S. Foreign Service, the U.S. Information Agency, AID, the Peace Corps and the Foreign Agricultural Service. A brief job title appears, date arrived in country they are assigned, and their civil service grade.

*Knowing Where to Look: The Ultimate Guide to Research*. Lists numerous ideas on using libraries for research.

*The National Yellow Book of Funeral Directors*. Contains names, addresses and telephone numbers of most funeral homes and directors in the United States. Lists information by city.

*Newspapers in Microfilm: United States*. A helpful reference for locating newspapers stored on microfilm. Published by the Library of Congress.

*Peterson's Guide to Four-year Colleges or Accredited Institutions of Post Secondary Education*. A useful guide to obtain addresses of college alumni associations or college libraries.

*Who's Who in America*. This series of books contain thousands of names and information on prominent people.

# Glossary

**Alias**
A fictitious name assumed by an individual.

**Amended Birth Certificate**
A document that replaces an original birth certificate. When a child is legally adopted an amended birth certificate is issued and the original is sealed.

**Archive**
A place where historical documents are stored.

**Armed Forces**
The armed forces are composed of the Air Force, Army, Coast Guard, Marine Corps and the Navy.

**Birth Certificate**
An official document issued by a government agency that indicates the date and place of birth, and name of an individual. Names of the parents and hospital are usually listed.

**Census**
An official count of the population in a geographical area. It also collects demographic information about the people such as age, sex, income, etc. Censuses are conducted by the appropriate government agencies usually every 10 years.

**Civil Service Employee**
An employee of the federal, state or local government who is not a member of the armed forces.

**Credit Report**
A report of an individual's credit history, including records of commercial and financial accounts. This information is not available to the general public.

**Database/File**
An organized collection of information; may be maintained and accessed by computer.

**Death Certificate**
An official document issued by a government agency confirming the date, place, and cause of an individual's death. May also include marital status, address at time of death, informant's name, veteran status, and survivors.

**Drivers License**
A permit to operate a motor vehicle, normally issued by each state government. A license may contain an individual's name, address, physical description, and the permit number or Social Security number.

**Fair Credit Reporting Act**
A federal law created to protect the credit information of an individual. Only businesses with a valid reason may obtain credit information.

**Freedom of Information Act**
A federal law requiring the U.S. government executive branch agencies and the armed forces to release information to the public upon request, unless exempted by privacy or national security reasons.

**Genealogical Library**
A library that specializes in family history information.

**Hit**
The successful result of a computer search; e.g., obtaining a name and correct address after entering a Social Security number.

**Identifying Information**
Any information used to identify and locate someone, such as: name, address, Social Security number, service number, date of birth, parents' names, etc.

**Legal Name**
The name on a person's birth certificate and other records and documents.

**Locator Service**
A company that locates people using information contained in records and databases.

**Military Locator**
The office on each base or post that has the names and units of assignment of all military personnel at that installation. The locator provides information to the general public.

**National Archives**
The depositories of historical documents of the federal government. The National Personnel Records Center is part of the National Archives.

**National Telephone Directory**
Any of the CD-ROMs or websites that contain phone numbers and addresses gathered from public phone directories.

**Newspaper Archives**
A collection of published newspapers.

**Open Records Act**
The laws outlining the information that may be released from official records maintained by state and local government agencies.

**Privacy Act**
The federal law designed to protect an individual's constitutional right to privacy. The law also allows disclosure to an individual of information the federal government maintains on that person.

**Service Number**
The unique number assigned to a person who served in the armed forces either on active duty, in the reserves, or National Guard. Service numbers were used from WW I to 1974.

**Social Security Number**
The unique nine-digit number assigned to citizens of the United States by the Social Security Administration. In reality, this number is a person's national identity number.

**The Uniformed Services**
The Uniformed Services are composed of the armed forces, the Public Health Service, and the National Oceanic and Atmospheric Administration.

**URL (Uniform Resource Locator)**
An address that a web browser uses to locate, retrieve and display a document.

**VA Claim Number**
The number assigned by the Department of Veterans Affairs when a veteran makes a claim for benefits. Since 1973, this number is the veteran's Social Security number.

**Veteran**
A person who has served on active duty in one or more of the armed forces. See "armed forces."

**Vital Records**
Birth and death certificates, marriage licenses, divorce and annulment decrees.

# About the Authors

Lt. Col. Richard S. Johnson (Ret) retired after serving 28 years in the U.S. Army working with personnel records and management, military postal operations, and automated data processing. He processed military records and ran two army locators, which turned him into an expert at locating people in the military. When the Vietnam veteran retired in 1979, he kept up his people-finding skills in civilian life.

In 1988 he shared his extensive knowledge and research on methods of locating current and former servicemen and women in the first edition of this book. He later wrote *Secrets of Finding Unclaimed Money* and *How to Find Anyone Who Is or Has Been in the Military.*

After his retirement, Dick teamed up with his daughter, Debra Johnson Knox, to form Military Information Enterprises, which publishes books and is a licensed private detective agency in Texas and South Carolina. Debra Knox is a licensed private investigator.

Debra was quite skeptical when her father first approached her in 1987 about forming a company to publish books about locating people. But now, almost 15 years later, she admits there is nothing else she would rather do. Helping reunite people is very rewarding.

Debra Knox lives with her family in South Carolina. Lt. Col. Richard Johnson passed away in February of 1999.

*Secrets of Finding Unclaimed Money*

Richard S. Johnson again shows us how to search—this time for unclaimed money. His expertise in locating people has brought him into a new field: heir searching.

Billions of dollars are in state unclaimed property offices, private companies, and life insurance proceeds just waiting for the rightful owner to come forward. However, many people are not aware of these funds or how easy it is to search and claim their money.

Billions of unclaimed dollars are in:

- Bank accounts
- Life insurance proceeds
- Retirement funds
- Stocks and bonds
- Dividend checks
- Security deposits
- Trust funds
- Tax refunds
- Savings bonds
- Employment checks

Discover how to:

- Find out if you or your family is due any unclaimed money from estates, the government, or businesses.
- Make money by locating the rightful owners of estates and other unclaimed money.

Lists are provided of all the resources you'll need:

- The unclaimed property offices in all 50 states.
- Federal agencies holding unclaimed money.
- Financial organizations with unclaimed money.

Richard S. Johnson, the author, is a professional heir searcher who has helped hundreds of people claim money they never knew existed.

*How To Locate Anyone Who Is or Has Been in the Military*
*Armed Forces Locator Guide*
*8th Edition*

Co-author Lt. Col. Richard S. Johnson (dec.) was the foremost expert in the nation on locating people with a military connection. His daughter and co-author, Debra Johnson Knox, is a licensed private investigator. Over 90,000 copies of this book have been sold and readers have located thousands of people. The 8th edition is completely revised, updated and expanded. A foreword is provided by General William Westmoreland.

This book contains directories of:

- U.S. Military Installations
- U.S. Base/Post Locators
- Air Force, Army, and Fleet Post Offices
- U.S. Navy and Coast Guard Ships
- Military and Veterans Organizations
- Military Unit Reunion Associations

Here is some of the valuable information included:

- How to obtain unit of assignment, home address and telephone number of any member of the Air Force, Army, Coast Guard, Marine Corps, Navy, the Reserve Components, and National Guard.
- How to locate current, former or retired members of the armed forces or reserves.
- How to locate any of 25 million living veterans.
- How to obtain ship or unit histories.
- How anyone can obtain copies of official military personnel records of current, former or deceased military members.

New chapters include: Locating Women Veterans, Verifying a Veteran's Military Service, Locating Birth Parents Who Served in the Military, Military and Veteran's Internet Sites, and Case Studies.

# Bookstore

*They Also Served: Military Biographies of Uncommon Americans* by Scott Baron. A fascinating collection of over 500 condensed military biographies of extraordinary Americans. The people profiled are known for their achievements outside the military. Prominent in their fields, whether it be law, medicine or the arts, their one commonality is that when our country called, they answered. Many interesting stories, facts, and trivia fill this wonderful, patriotic book. 333 pages, $18.95.

*How to Locate Anyone Who Is or Has Been in the Military: Armed Forces Locator Guide* (8th Edition) by Lt. Col. Richard S. Johnson (Ret) and Debra Johnson Knox. Learn all conceivable means of locating current and former members of the Air Force, Army, Coast Guard, Marine Corps, Navy, Reserve and National Guard. New chapters in this updated and expanded edition include: Verifying Military Service, Locating Women Veterans, and Case Studies. 299 pages, $22.95.

*Secrets of Finding Unclaimed Money* by Richard S. Johnson. An experienced heir searcher reveals all the secrets of finding unclaimed money held by state unclaimed property offices, other state agencies and the federal government. He also teaches how to earn money by becoming a professional heir searcher. Includes sample forms and contracts. 182 pages, $11.95.

Please add $5.05 shipping/handling to all orders. Send to:

MIE Publishing
PO Box 17118
Spartanburg, SC 29301
(800) 937-2133, (864) 595-0813 Fax
*www.militaryusa.com*

# Notes

# Notes

# Notes

# Notes

# Notes

# Index